A Dorset Christmas

A JOLLY CHRISTMAS.

A Victorian Christmas card.

A Dorset Christmas

Compiled by
Fran and Geoff Doel

The History Press

To Dr Michael Baron, Birkbeck College, with many thanks.

Front cover: Detail of a roddick (robin) from the Sherborne Missal. Add.74236, page 32. By permission of the British Library.

First published in 2005 by
Tempus Publishing

Reprinted in 2008 by
The History Press
The Mill, Brimscombe Port,
Stroud, Gloucestershire, GL5 2QG
www.thehistorypress.co.uk

British Library Cataloguing in Publication Data.
A catalogue record for this book is available from the British Library.

ISBN 978 0 7524 3579 4

Typesetting and origination by
Tempus Publishing Limited
Printed in the UK by CPI Bookmarque, Croydon, CR0 4TD

Contents

The Authors

Fran and Geoff Doel are sessional lecturers in literature, medieval and cultural studies for the Universities of Kent and Sussex and Birkbeck College. Geoff has a PhD on Thomas Hardy and Fran an MA in Medieval Studies. They have published nine books, including Christmas anthologies on Kent and Sussex.

Acknowledgements and Sources

'A Christmas Frolic', *Dorset County Chronicle*, December 1828; synopsis in Jo Draper's *Regency, Riot and Reform*.

'A Draft of the Dorset' by Sir Frederick Treves, *The Dorset Year Book*, 1918-19.

'Christmas Charities at Bere Regis and Blandford', information from Hutchins' *History* and Jo Draper in *Thomas Hardy's England*.

'Christmas Earthquake at Lyme Regis, 1839', 'The Mighty Landslip' by Laurence Dopson, *Dorset County Journal*, 1947.

'Christmas Comforts', *The Southern Times*, 1939.

'Christmas in the County Hospital, 1913', *Dorset County Chronicle and Somersetshire Gazette*, 1914.

'Christmas in the Workhouse', *Dorset County Chronicle and Somersetshire Gazette*, 1903.

'Christmas in Wartime', *The Southern Times*, 1939.

'Christmas Poaching on the Lulworth Estate', information from Jo Draper's *Regency, Riot and Reform*.

'How Dorchester Keeps Christmas', *Dorset County Chronicle and Somersetshire Gazette*, 1914.

'Memories of Christmas by M.A. Roberts', *Dorset County Journal*, 1950.

'Mr Smith's Public Ball in The Antelope' from 'Before You Were Born', *The Southern Times*, 1939.

'Robin Redbreast: The Bird of the Christmas Card' by Denys Watkins-Pritchard, *Hants and Dorset Magazine*, Christmas Number, 1954.

'The Bockhampton Band Versus the Fordington Mummers', *Dorset County Chronicle*, 24 January 1928, quoted in Michael Millgate's *Thomas Hardy: His Career as a Novelist*.

'The Christmas Thrift Club' by John Eastwood from 'Winter' in the *Hampshire and Dorset Magazine*, 1957.

'The Hungry Forties', Parliamentary Commission, 1843, quoted in Joe Bettey's *Rural Life in Wessex*.

'The Kissing Bough' by Laurence Whistler, *Dorset County Magazine*, 1948.

'The White Donkey' by Benjamin Pond, *Dorset County Magazine*, 1969.

'Village Pantomime' by D. Cresswell, *Dorset County Journal*, 1951.

Front cover illustration by permission of the British Library, Add.74236, page 382.

All unattributed items are by Geoff and Fran Doel.

Our thanks to the staff of the Dorchester Public Library and Dorset History Centre and Record Office, and to Katherine Burton at Tempus for her help and encouragement.

Introduction

Christmas celebrations are a fusion of midwinter, solstitial and new year rituals and celebrations with the religious celebration of the birth of Christ. Their fusion is deliberate in that the early Church specifically chose the season of pre-Christian celebrations – the Yule festivities of Northern Europe, the Roman feasts of the Saturnalia, Kalends and the Unconquered Sun, and the eastern cult (adopted by Rome) of the birth of Mithras. Both elements are social in that they involve the celebrations of community groups. The interaction and the tension between religious and social ritual is dramatised in the works of Dorset's greatest son, Thomas Hardy. Although an agnostic, Hardy was steeped in the Bible and in Church ritual, and would have liked to believe in religion and/or the supernatural, as his exquisite poem 'The Oxen' makes clear. The Mellstock and Longpuddle Quires in Hardy's fiction show the social and religious problems encountered by musicians who played both sacred and secular music. Strangely enough, Dorset's second greatest poet, William Barnes, who became a church minister, focuses on the secular side of Christmas in the poems included in this anthology.

Dorset was once part of the Anglo-Saxon kingdom of Wessex and these elements had already fused into extensive Midwinter celebrations when King Alfred was taken by surprise by a Viking attack during his feasting at Chippenham in 878. Clearly, too many mince pies and wild boar sausages nearly lost Alfred his kingdom and his diet soon declined to burnt cakes!

Liturgical Christmas celebrations in Dorset focused on the great religious Anglo-Saxon foundations such as Abbotsbury (founded in the mid-eleventh century), Milton Abbas (founded 935), Shaftesbury (nunnery founded in late ninth century by Alfred), Sherborne (see of the Bishop of Wessex from 705) and Wimborne (founded as a nunnery in 705), all of which flourished into the Middle Ages. We have featured the Sherborne Missal in this book as a famous example of illuminated work from Dorset, but the Shaftesbury Psalter from the shrine of the martyred King Edward, the Anglo-Saxon king murdered at Corfe, also celebrates the Christmas feast days in text and illustrated symbol. This was thought to have been illuminated by a nun at the abbey in around 1130 and it gives details of services for Matins and Vespers on the feasts of St Nicholas (6 December), the Conception of Mary (8 December), St Thomas (21 December), St Stephen (26 December), St John the Evangelist (27 December), the Holy Innocents (28 December) and St Silvester (31 December).

We have included a number of traditional practices whose connections with the Christian Christmas are, at the most, tenuous: mummers' plays, the ashen faggot, the Dorset Ooser and hobby horse and divination practices. Ghosts and ghost stories are traditional at Christmas, so we have included a couple of these. Also on the social side, there are the accounts of Christmas balls, pantomimes and present-giving, and of the dedicated efforts of police, postal workers, soldiers and the fire service at this time of year. Smuggling, wrecking and poaching over Christmas takes us to the windy side of the law and we print a sermon bravely attacking the looting of wrecks in the heart of the Chesil country. Some bizarre and interesting events have been included because they occurred over the Christmas period, but these often give a wider insight into the celebrations. For example, the Lyme Regis earthquake article shows how the farmer and the families of his employees got together on Christmas Eve.

We hope this collection of stories is, to a small extent, able to convey the warmth, distinctiveness and vitality of Dorset people and Dorset Christmases past and present.

Fran and Geoff Doel
April 2005

A Christmas card from Palmer's Brewery, Bridport, operational since 1794. It brews a distinctive ale for the midwinter season – Tally Ho! – which is 'strong, dark and nutty'.

Chris'mas Invitation
By William Barnes

William Barnes (1801-1886), the famous poet of the Dorset dialect, spent his early life in the Vale of Blackmore and then worked as a solicitor's clerk in Dorchester from 1818 to 1823. He then took up teaching, first running a school at Mere and then moving back to run a Dorchester school in 1835 and helping to found the Dorset County Museum. He then graduated in Divinity at St John's College, Cambridge in 1850 and became Rector of Came in 1862. Barnes was a prolific writer of poetry, reviews and non-fictional articles. He wrote poetry both in what he called 'national English' ('Linden Lea' is a famous example) and in the dialect. His Poems of Rural Life in the Dorset Dialect *(1844) was highly praised and Barnes became internationally recognised as a philologist. 'Chris'mas Invitation', from this collection, anticipates Christmas festivities in the Vale of Blackmore, which are to include everyone telling a story and singing a song. Lots of ale is to be imbibed and games such as Blind Man's Buff played.*

> Come down to-morrow night; an, mind
> Don't leave thy fiddle-bag behind;
> We'll sheake a lag, an' drink a cup
> O'eale, to keep wold Chris'mas up.
>
> An' let thy sister teake thy earm,
> The walk won't do her any harm;
> There's noo dirt now to spweil her frock,
> The ground's a-vroze so hard's a rock.

You won't meet any stranger's feace,
But only neighbours o'the pleace,
An' Stowe, an' Combe; an' two or dree
Vrom uncle's up at Rookery.

An' thou wu'lt vind a rwosy feace,
An' peair ov eyes so black as sloos,
The prettiest woones in all the pleace, –
I'm sure I needen tell thee whose.

We got a back-bran, dree girt logs
So much as dree ov us can car;
We'll put 'em up athirt the dogs,
An meake a vier to the bar.

An' ev'ry woone shall tell his teale,
An' ev'ry woone shall zing his zong,
An' ev'ry woone wull drink his eale
To love an' frien'ship all night long.

We'll snap the tongs, we'll have a ball,
We'll shake the house, we'll lift the ruf,
We'll romp an' meake the maidens squall,
A'catchen o'm at blind-man's buff.

Zoo come to-morrow night; an' mind,
Don't leave thy fiddle-bag behind;
We'll sheake a lag, an' drink a cup
O'eale, to keep wold Chris'mas up.

The Hungry Forties

Evidence from Rachel Hayward to the
1843 Parliamentary Commission
Cited in Joe Bettey's Rural Life in Wessex

Roughly at the same time that Barnes was writing the previous poem, and in the same part of Dorset and the same time of year, we see the contrasting reality of the lifestyle of a lower class – the labourers. Dorset was notorious for low wages and overcrowded and insanitary living conditions in the 'hungry forties' and a Parliamentary Commission was appointed to investigate in 1843. In December, the following statement was taken from Rachel Hayward, the wife of John Hayward, a farm labourer of Stourpaine. The family is very dependent on the money the daughters bring in from the cottage industry of buttoning (common in the Vale of Blackmore at that period) and for food on potatoes.

There are eleven of us in our family – myself, my husband, three daughters and six sons. We have two rooms, one down stairs and the other up stairs over it. We all sleep in the bedroom. My husband gets 8s or 7s a week; my two eldest daughters get about 3s 6d a week at buttoning, and three of my boys get 5s a week together; in all about 16s 6d a week. We have sixteen and a half lugs of potato-ground on which we grow potatoes and few vegetables; for that we pay 7s 7d a year rent. We pay 1s a week for the cottage, and coal and wood cost us 1s 8d a week at this time of year. We get three quarters of a hundredweight of coal a week. I buy besides, every week three quarters of a pound of soap, one ounce of tea, half a pound of bacon. I reckon we eat a pound of bread each day; that with potatoes gives us enough. My three boys that are out at work went out at nine years old.

Dorset cottage
interior,
Hermann Lea,
c. 1890.

Thomas Hardy's Christmases

From The Life of Thomas Hardy *by Florence Hardy*

*

Thomas Hardy (1840-1928) is synonymous with traditional Dorset life, though he never refers to Dorset in his fictional work, preferring the geographically wider and more ancient concept of Wessex. However, many of his novels, short stories and poems are firmly located in recognisable Dorset locations to which he often gives fictional, but distinguishable, names.

Hardy came from a musical family: his grandfather founded the Stinsford Quire of stringed musicians and boy singers, to which Hardy's father and uncle also belonged, and they played regularly in the West Gallery at Stinsford church on Sundays and Christmas Days until just after Hardy's birth. The Hardys also ran a dance band which outlived the ecclesiastical performers and Hardy frequently played fiddle with his father at local dances as a boy and young man. The rich religious and secular experiences and adventures of the Hardy musicians (particularly at Christmas) are recounted through the fictional Mellstock band, and one or two other bands, in Under the Greenwood Tree *and several short stories and poems.*

Hardy knew the steps of the country dances, he saw his Sparks cousins perform a Mummers Play at Puddletown (he may have taken a part) and he is remembered as singing the folksong 'Dame Durden' at a local party. Class consciousness in this writer aspiring to middle classes status initially made Hardy reticent about his personal involvement in local traditional culture, despite the thematic and dramatic way he uses customs, dances and songs in his novels, and his anxiousness to accurately record a rich and passing way of life. But in his later days he gradually realised that it was becoming quite fashionable to

own to relatively humble authentic origins and he revealed more of his personal involvement with his own culture.

Anxious to avoid an official biography, Hardy dictated his autobiography to his second wife, Florence, and told her to complete it after his death and publish it under her name; most of the style is unmistakably Hardy's. This work makes numerous references to Hardy's enjoyment of celebrating Christmas, and a selection of these are drawn from it below.

It was natural that with the imitativeness of a boy he should have at an early age attempted to perform on the violin, and under his father's instruction was soon able to tweedle from notation some hundreds of jigs and country-dances that he found in his father's and grandfather's old books. (1848-52)

So little Thomas Hardy played sometimes at village weddings, at one of which the bride, all in white, kissed him in her intense pleasure at the dance; once at a New Year's Eve party in the house of the tailor who had breeched him; also in farmer's parlours; and on another occasion at a homestead where he was stopped by his hostess clutching his bow-arm at the end of a three-quarter-hour's unbroken footing to his notes by twelve tireless couples in the favourite country-dance of 'The New-Rigged Ship'. The matron had done it lest he should 'burst a bloodvessel', fearing the sustained exertion to be too much for a boy of thirteen or fourteen.

Among the queer occurrences accompanying these merry minstrellings may be described one that happened when he was coming home with his father at three in the morning from a gentleman-farmer's house where he had been second violin to his senior's first for six or seven

The Cottage, Higher Bockhampton, where Hardy was born.

hours, his father for some reason having had a generous wish to oblige the entertainers to the full. It was bitterly cold, and the moon glistened bright upon the encrusted snow, amid which they saw motionless in the hedge what appeared to be a white human figure without a head. The boy, being very tired, with finger-tips tingling from pressing the strings, was for passing the ghastly sight quickly, but the elder went up to the object, which proved to be a very tall thin man in a long white smock-frock, leaning against the bank in a drunken stupor, his head hanging forward so low that at a distance he had seemed to have no head at all. Hardy senior, seeing the danger of leaving the man where he might be frozen to death, awoke him after much exertion, and they supported him to a cottage near, where he lived, and pushed him in through the door, their ears being greeted as they left with a stream of abuse from the man's wife, which was also vented upon her unfortunate husband, whom she promptly knocked down. Hardy's father grimly remarked that it might have been as well to leave him where he was, to take his chance of being frozen to death. (1852-54)

...when, returning from Cornwall on a fine December noontide (being New Year's Eve 1873-74), he opened on Plymouth Hoe a copy of the *Cornhill* that he had brought at the station, and there to his surprise saw his story placed at the beginning of the magazine, with a striking illustration, the artist being – also to his surprise – not a man but a woman, Miss Helen Paterson. (1873-74)

Hardy was returning from Christmas at his fiancée's at St Juliot's Rectory and the 'story' is the first instalment of Far From the Madding Crowd.

They [Hardy and Emma] spent Christmas with Hardy's father and mother; and while there his father told them that when he was a boy the hobby-horse was still a Christmas amusement. On one occasion the village band of West Stafford was at Mr Floyer's (the landowner) at a party, where among other entertainments was that of the said hobby-horse. One of the servants was terrified death-white at the sight of it running about, and rushed into an adjoining dark room where the band's violoncello was lying, entering with such force as to knock off the neck of the instrument. (1876)

On the last day of the year Hardy's father wrote, saying that ... he had 'drunk both their healths in gin and rhubarb wine, with hopes that they would live to see many and many a New Year's day'. (1878)

The year was wound up by Hardy and his wife at a ball at Lady Wimborne's, Canford Manor ... Lord Wimborne in a conversation about the house complained that it was rendered damp by the miller below penning the water for grinding, and, on Hardy's suggesting the removal of the mill, his host amused him by saying that was out of the question, because the miller paid him £50 a year in rent. However that might have been Hardy felt glad the old mill was to remain, having as great a repugnance to pulling down a mill where (to use his own words) they ground food for the body, as to pulling down a church where they ground food for the soul. (1881)

[Note by Hardy] December 23. There is what we used to call 'The Birds' Bedroom' in the plantation at Bockhampton. Some large hollies grow among leafless ash, oak, birch, etc. At this time of year the birds select the hollies for roosting in, and at dusk noises not unlike the creaking of withy-chairs arise, with a busy rustling as of people going to bed in a lodging-house; accompanied by sundry shakings, adjustings, and pattings, as if they were making their beds vigorously before turning in... On the eve of the New Year 1884 Hardy planted some trees on his new property at Max Gate, Dorchester. (1884)

[Note by Hardy] December 31. To St Peter's belfry [Dorchester] to the New-Year's-Eve ringing. The night-wind whiffed in through the louvres as the men prepared the mufflers with tar-twine and pieces of horse-cloth. Climbed over the bells to fix the mufflers. I climbed with them and looked into the tenor bell: it is worn into a bright pit where the clapper has struck so many years, and the clapper is battered with its many blows.

The ringers now put their coats and waistcoats and hats upon the chimes and clock and stand to. Old John is fragile, as if the bell would pull him up rather than he pull the rope down, his neck being withered and white

as his white neckcloth. But his manner is severe as he says, 'Tenor out?'
One of the two tenor men gently eases the bell forward – that fine old
E flat, my father's admiration, unsurpassed in metal all the world over
– and answers, 'Tenor's out'. Then old John tells them to 'Go!' and they
start. Through long practice he rings with the least possible movement
of his body, though the youngest ringers – strong, dark-haired men
with ruddy faces – soon perspire with their exertions. The red, green
and white sallies bolt up through the holes like rats between the huge
beams overhead.

The grey stones of the fifteenth century masonry have many of their
joints mortarless, and are carved with many initials and dates. On the sill
of one louvred window stands a great pewter pot with a hinged cover
and engraved: 'For the use of the ringers 16-'. (1884)

[Note by Hardy] Dec. 31. A silent New Year's Eve – no bell, or band,
or voice … Jan. 7. On New Year's Eve and day I sent off five copies of
the magazine containing a story of mine, and three letters – all eight to
friends by way of New Year's greetings and good wishes. *Not a single
reply*. Mem.: never send New Year's letter &c. again. (1887-8)

[Note by Hardy] New Year's Eve. Looked out of doors just before
twelve, and was confronted by the toneless white of the snow spread in
front, against which stood the row of pines breathing out: ''Tis no better
with us than with the rest of creation, you see!' I could not hear the
church bells. (1890)

He spent Christmas at Max Gate as usual, receiving the carol-
singers there on Christmas Eve, where 'though quite modern, with a

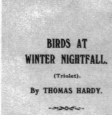

Hardy's poetic and visual image of a snowbound Max Gate, from *Poems of the Past and Present* (1901).

harmonium, they made a charming picture with their lanterns under the trees, the rays diminishing away in the winter mist'. On New Year's Eve it was calm, and they stood outside the door listening to the muffled peal from the tower of Fordington St. George. (1893)

In December Time's Laughingstocks was published, and Hardy was in London, coming back as usual with a choking sore throat which confined him to his bed till the New Year, on the eve of which at twelve o'clock he crouched by the fire and heard in the silence of the night the ringing of the muffled peal down the chimney of his bedroom from the neighbouring church of St. George. (1909)

GREETINGS - - - from
Mr. and Mrs. THOMAS HARDY

Max Gate.
Dorchester.   Xmas. 1921

The dog Wessex did not always give warm greetings!

Thomas and Florence Hardy's
Christmas card, 1921.

[Note by Hardy] December 31. New Year's Eve. Went to bed at eleven.
East wind. No bells heard. Slept in the New Year, as did also those 'out
there'. (1917)

On Christmas night the carol-singers and mummers came to Max Gate
as they had promised, the latter performing the *Play of Saint George*, just
as he had seen it performed in his childhood. (1920)

On the last day but one of the year Mr and Mrs G. Bernard Shaw and
Colonel T. E. Lawrence lunched with the Hardys and spent several hours
with them.

[Note by Hardy] 31. New Year's Eve. Did not sit up. Heard the bells in the evening.

January 2. Attended Frederick Treves's funeral at St. Peter's. Very wet day. Sad procession to the cemetery. Casket in a little white grave. (1923-4)

[Note by Hardy] Dec. 31. New Year's Eve. F. and I sat up. Heard on the wireless various features of New Year's Eve in London: dancing at the Albert Hall, Big Ben striking twelve, singing Auld Lang Syne, God Save the King, Marseillaise, hurrahing. (1925)

St Peter's church in Dorchester, which was restored by Hardy. This was where he attended the New Year bell-ringing.

He continued to come downstairs to sit for a few hours daily, until Christmas-day. After that he came downstairs no more.

On December 26 he said that he had been thinking of the Nativity and of the Massacre of the Innocents, and his wife read to him the gospel accounts... He remarked that there was not a grain of evidence that the gospel story was true in any detail.

As the year ended a window in the dressing-room adjoining his bedroom was opened that he might hear the bells, as that had always pleased him. (1927)

Florence Hardy, 'author' of *The Life of Thomas Hardy*.

The First Policeman at Swanage

By William Masters Hardy

From Old Swanage, or Purbeck Past and Present, 1910

✳

Hardy is writing about mob violence directed against the provincial police force at Christmastime in Swanage in the early 1850s. In the early eighteenth century, the guardians of the English public were the Charleys or watchmen who did a nightly street patrol but they were often ridiculed as being too decrepit or incompetent to be effective. In the mid-eighteenth century, magistrate Henry Fielding (the famous novelist) was appointed at Bow Street, London. It was he who organised the parish constables into squads in 1749 for the detection of malefactors – the squads were officially termed the Bow Street Runners ('runner' being the term for a magistrate's officer). In 1782 the Bow Street Patroles (a small force of armed police) were added to the Runners. Later, Sir Robert Peel would combine the patroles, runners, parish constables and Charleys in London to become his new police force – the Metropolitan Police, affectionately known as the Peelers. Later Acts of Parliament extended Peel's system to the towns and boroughs of England and Wales and then to the counties. Note that even at that period the dark blue uniform of the policeman had already inspired the nickname 'man in blue' as well as Peeler.

The recent increase of the police force at Swanage by the appointment by the Dorset Standing Joint Committee of an extra constable on the recommendation of the Home Office reminds one of the rough experiences of the first policeman stationed in the town. At that time,

The Swanage lock-up (photograph by Geoff Doel).

upwards of 50 years ago, Swanage was by no means such a model of law and order as it is now. The inhabitants, always sturdy and independent, were not so well bred and polished in their manners as half a century of development, education and increasing intercourse with visitors have since combined to make them. Indeed, several of the natives were rude and lawless, and the peace was not infrequently broken. On one occasion, when the second Earl of Eldson was driving through the street in his carriage, a boy flung an iron hoop through the carriage window. His Lordship, in the absence of any officially appointed preserver of the peace, took the law into his own hands, and getting out of the carriage with as much dignity as possible under the circumstances, he boxed the youthful delinquent's ears.

27

With a view to the protection of property and the better order and government of the town, Mr John Mowlem exerted himself to get a policeman stationed here, and, to facilitate the arrangement, he contributed ten shillings a week out of his own pocket towards the officer's pay. The sergeant and constables of the Dorset County Constabulary now policing the district are generally treated with respect and politeness. They are by no means unpopular, and are seldom hindered or molested in the discharge of sometimes disagreeable duties. But it was very different in 1851. Like most communities who lived somewhat isolated from the great body of their fellow men, Swanage folk, or at least a certain section of them, at that time regarded strangers with a jealous and suspicious eye, and the rougher element resented the intrusion of this policeman as in the nature of an insult and an injury. They knew that he had been brought there to keep a watch upon them, and to pay attention to their morals and manners; but, like naughty children, they did not desire to amend, but wanted to have their own way as before. So after a while a conspiracy was organised to 'make it hot' for *Robertus Primus* (i.e. Sir Robert Peel).

Mobbed on Christmas Eve

Various petty annoyances and vexations came to a head on Christmas Eve, 1851, when at midnight a body of rough set upon the man in blue. They mobbed him and nearly killed him, pressing him hard against the door of Mr Phineas Melmoth's house near the New Inn. I think that Mr Devil Drink was responsible for the brutal and savage violence of this assault. I must now introduce the heroine of the story. Everybody has heard about Brave Dame Mary of Corfe Castle; but I wish to let my readers know that Swanage had a 'Brave Dame Mary'. With womanly feeling, but masculine courage and presence of mind she showed on this occasion what stuff she was made of. Hearing a loud scuffle outside the street door and stifled cries of 'Murder, murder' from the half suffocated victim, Mrs Mary Melmoth, whose husband and children had gone to bed, and who was about to follow them, unlocked the door, without a moment's hesitation and drew the poor 'Bobby' into the house, the scene almost reproducing that which Holy Writ records to have taken place in the doomed city of Sodom, when Lot, almost torn to pieces by the enraged Sodomites, was drawn inside the door by the angels. And truly the role performed by Mrs Melmoth must have appeared to the rescued man quite that of a 'ministering angel'. The unfortunate 'Peeler' was assisted into Mrs Melmoth's house by a Mr Butler, who helped him in dressing his wounds and afterwards saw him home. The mob, half ashamed by this apparition, and half frightened at the possible consequences of their action, fled precipitately, leaving the policeman in a sorry state. His gracious and pitiful rescuer tended his injuries and took every care of him.

Presentation to the Heroine

The outrage on the policeman, and how he was saved from probable murder by Mrs Melmoth, was next day the talk of the town, and soon afterwards the inhabitants, in commemoration of the event and in recognition of the lady's brave deed, subscribed and presented her with a large silver-gilt cup with the following engraved on it:

Presented
To
Mrs Phineas Melmoth

29

By
The Inhabitants of Swanage
As a
Token of Admiration of Her Courage
On
Christmas Eve, 1851

The cup is still in the family and is highly cherished, and will continue to be while her descendants live. I may add that Mr Melmoth's father was Clerk of the Parish Church of St. Mary's for over 30 years. He had a powerful bass voice, which he used effectively in giving out the hymns, and thus he became known as Bass Jimmy. He had been in the Royal Navy in the Napoleonic Wars, and had fought under Lord Nelson. He served in the Battle of the Nile, 1798.

I am glad to say that the police and people get on much better together now than they did half a century ago.

An itinerant fiddler outside the Ship Hotel in Dorchester, drawn by Thomas Hardy.

Christmas Eve – A False Alarm, 1862
From the Dorset County Chronicle, *25 December 1862*

This is a rather unusual ironic article, but it does provide valuable insights into both mid-nineteenth-century Christmas Eve in Dorchester and the organisation of the fire services at the same period. The journalist clearly doesn't think much of his rival witness to the Yule log celebrations, a ballad writer and singer who seems to have a home printing press in Pig Lane and who sings and sells his wares in the street. The Dorset County Chronicle *writer attacks his rival in terms of class, appearance and literary merit, but he does dramatise the Duke of Sutherland and Captain Shaw entertaining a more charitable attitude to the ballad singer, which gives the piece a happy ending.*

The actual way in which the ballad singer triggered the fire alarm by way of the beacons on Maumbury Rings, Maiden Castle and Poundbury is rather mysterious – presumably by the word 'fire' in one of his songs?

The Ancient Order of Druids dragging a Yule log is a delightful and typically Victorian confusion of Celtic and Germanic folk custom, the Yule log being from the Germanic culture. The 'song' they are singing is in fact a verse from a poem, 'Hesperides' by the seventeenth-century Devon poet Robert Herrick, and shows that this is a middle-class antiquarian revival, part perhaps of the new Merrie England culture. However, there was a Dorset tradition of the Yule log which survived to this period, described by John Udal in a contribution to Notes and Queries *in December 1880 and summarised in his book* Dorsetshire Folk-Lore:*

It was customary in many farmhouses on Christmas Eve for a large block of wood to be brought into the kitchen, and an immense fire

31

having been made up, the farm labourers would come in and sit round it, or as many as were able would crowd into the chimney corner, and drink beer and cider. This was what was usually called a Christmas 'brown'.

A queer scene occurred in Dorchester last evening. It is not generally known, perhaps, that on Christmas Eve the Metropolitan Fire Brigade had made preparations so extensive for the extinction of fires – and particularly of the fires of Genius... A Lodge of Ancient Druids having dragged a yule log, long marked out in Col. Dawson Damer's plantations at Came, to some convenient spot, were kindling it with great solemnity, singing:

THE YULE LOG.

A Victorian illustration of the Yule Log.

Come bring with a noise,
My merry merry boys,
The Christmas log to the firing;
While my good dame she
Bids you all be free,
And drink to your heart's desiring.

The log being thus dragged in was lighted with a brand saved from the previous year's burning; when a low-bred shabby farming-looking man, with a goose's foot sticking out of his hat like the foot out of a Christmas pie, commonly known in Dorchester as 'The Goose' rambled towards the scene of the action. The man, though not a recognised member of the Press, pretends to grind a gaunt, squeaking, wretched little organ of his own in the rural back settlement of Pig Lane; and in this instance he made the mistake of fancying he could convert the occasion of the Yule fire into a paragraph. He made the attempt, and gained 'the Goose Pie' as usual; for nothing of his story being intelligible save the word 'fire' – up went the signal rockets from Maumbury Rings, Maiden Castle, and Poundbury in rapid succession; and at longer intervals along the outline of the Dorset heights might be seen extending the warning signals, which at length brought down express Capt. Shaw and the Duke of Sutherland to see what could be done. The first of official and amateur firemen started by special train from Waterloo Bridge ... The train, though first and special, took long to arrive.

It was near midnight when the intrepid strangers reached our Chestnut-walk environed town. Wassailers were abundant; and the sounds of mirth and revelry burst from almost every lighted abode. In the streets there was one wretched solitary object, who unless it had been for the inexplicable tinglings he maintained with a muffin-bell,

33

which he carried in one hand, whilst he clutched some crumpled and dirty sheets of paper in the other, might have been mistaken for a singer of Christmas Carols. But the miserere which the poor man chanted with dirge like monotony, was more akin to those begging petitions published ... at this season of gifts, donations and Christmas boxes. [*The Duke of Sutherland and Captain Shaw spot him.*]

'After all', observed the gallant hero of a hundred fires to the noble Duke, 'after all your Grace, there is a fire here, that is the fire of Genius.'

'Yes', replied his Grace, 'that sort is only to be extinguished with twopenny, but on Christmas Eve, I suppose we are bound to do it.'

'Let us do it and be off', said the practical Captain.

Whatever may have been the unwanted guerdon bestowed on the lonely singer of our deserted Dorchester streets by these two illustrious visitors, he proffered them in exchange his whole stock in hand. But after the comment himself had made upon these wares, acceptance of them was declined, and the Muffineer made off with them as fast as his legs would carry him in the direction of the Antelope Tap. There an attempt was made to light with them the pipes of several people assembled, but they would not even burn. They only smouldered miserably, and nearly suffocated the whole neighbourhood. Thus 'the alarm of fire' was in every way a false one; and the two disenchanted visitors as they sped back to the metropolis in their special return train, fully agreed that there was no danger of fire whatever from *goose dripping*.

The Oxen

By Thomas Hardy

✳

Thomas Hardy is unusual is being both a great novelist and a great poet. Hardy had an extensive experience and knowledge of Dorset traditional culture which is used thematically and dramatically in his writings.

Hardy was intensely aware of and fascinated by the seasonal pattern of rural life and Christmas was a favourite time for him – many of his poems, novels and short stories celebrate the activities and traditions of this special season. 'The Oxen' is emblematic of Hardy's love of traditional beliefs, his sadness at not being able to believe in Christianity despite being so attached to many of its rituals and his longing for a supernatural experience to give a window on the mystery of life. Even as an agnostic of seventy-five, his attitude to the tradition of the kneeling animals on Christmas Eve is one of 'hoping it might be so'.

The interesting concept that oxen and other creatures kneel at midnight on Christmas Eve (or often on Old Christmas Eve – i.e. ignoring the changes to the calendar in the eighteenth century as many folk traditions in the west of England did) to celebrate the nativity is widespread in Wessex. John Brand's influential Popular Antiquities of Great Britain *(1870) talks of the tradition in Devon and Somerset:*

At twelve o'clock at night on Christmas Eve, the oxen in their stalls are always found on their knees, as in an attitude of devotion; and that (which is still more singular) since the alteration of the style they continue to do this only on the Eve of old Christmas Day. An honest countryman ... informed me, 1790, that he once, with some others, made a trial of the truth of the above, and watching several oxen in their stalls at the above time, at twelve o'clock at night, they observed the two oldest oxen only fall upon their knees, and, as he expressed it ... make 'a cruel moan like Christian creatures'.

The tradition has been traced back as far as a Latin poem of the fifteenth century by Sannazarius which mentions an ox and an ass kneeling at the nativity.

This perfect, simple yet profound poem was published in The Times *during the First World War on 24 December 1915. It was subsequently published in*

Hardy's volume of poetry entitled Moments of Vision *and* Miscellaneous Verses *in 1917.*

Christmas Eve, and twelve of the clock
'Now they are all on their knees,'
An elder said as we sat in a flock
By the embers in hearthside ease.

We pictured the meek mild creatures where
They dwelt in their strawy pen,
Nor did it occur to one of us there
To doubt they were kneeling then.

So fair a fancy few would weave
In these years! Yet, I feel,
If someone said on Christmas Eve,
'Come; see the Oxen kneel!'

'In the lonely barton by yonder coomb
Our childhood used to know.'
I should go with him in the gloom,
Hoping it might be so.

Memories of Christmas
By M.A. Roberts

This article reflects the memories of girlhood visits to grandparents at Poole in the early twentieth century and incorporates her father's even earlier memories of Poole in the late nineteenth century. There is a detailed description of the children's Christmas presents and of the regular Christmas morning visit to Poole Park to see the monkeys, parrots, peacocks and swans. This is followed by a description of the turkey and Christmas pudding dinner, the turkey being cooked in the large oven of a local bakery. Finally the after-tea games are described.

We always went to Poole in Dorset for Christmas as a matter of course though the pleasure of anticipation never diminished.

One year we found a beautiful new restaurant on Waterloo station. A splendid fire glowed a welcome as we walked, in conscious luxury, over the thick carpet towards a table selected by my father. The white damask and silver, familiar enough at home, seemed to wear a romantic splendour in this spacious apartment. And the strange discovery of printed words, Southern Railway, in the middle of one's table napkin, marvellously woven into the linen, seemed to confirm our suspicion that we were approaching a world of marvel and magnificence.

We wore wide-brimmed cherry red beaver hats, navy blue coats and creamy white ermine muffs with three black tails on the front. We had fur necklets to match. Our best frocks that year were red velvet with cream point lace collars and cuffs. Black stockings ornamented with clocks and button boots with patent leather toe caps completed the ensemble. The care with which our mother prepared us for the kindly but discerning inspection of Grandma and the aunties only added to our sense of the importance of the occasion. My father's top-hat travelled in elegant and solitary state in a white silk-lined box of its own. What further evidence could we need of the honour due to the beloved relatives in Dorset?

A Victorian Christmas card.

On Christmas day itself we woke very early in the morning and realising, with shivers of excitement, the proximity of loaded stockings would fumble around in the darkness whispering and giggling. The grown-ups, after muffled injunctions from the next bedroom to go to sleep again, would resign themselves to the inevitable and bring the matches. At last the lamps were lit and placed in some safe spot. With awe and joy we each hoisted our own stocking over the brass rail of the bed. Father Christmas had come! We found pink sugar mice, chocolate animals, skilfully packed boxes of dolls furniture, a Japanese lady dolly with black hair and tiny white hands, tinkling musical boxes, coloured beads under a glass lid, tin trumpets, fur monkeys on elastic, nuts, apples and an orange. Amongst the fripperies there was always a 'sensible' present. Father Christmas, we were given to understand, took a balanced view of life! So white woollen gloves, goloshes, handkerchiefs and even my first little umbrella emerged from the black depths.

At last the mothers and aunties announced that it was time to dress so each member of the merry meeting departed to his or her own room. Our mother was most 'advanced' in believing that comfortable white sleeping suits, all in one piece, were preferable to night gowns. On Christmas morning these suits were a great advantage as somersaults of joy could be turned without endangering the properties.

Breakfast was a carefully circumscribed meal in view of the sugar mice and chocolate animals. Grandfather said grace.

After breakfast the proper presents, as distinct from the stockings, were given and received. My gift to our grandma was always a piece of my own handiwork; a black satin table centre embroidered with raised roses or pen painting on ribbon for curtain loops. It happened that I could sew at an early age and her pleased smile of approval was my reward.

Christmas presents.

During the morning we all trooped up to Poole Park. The weather always seemed to be mild and sunny but my father astonished us with stories of how he had skated on the lake by moonlight when he was young. Mysterious romance seemed to attach itself to this event. 'On the night of the news of the relief of Mafeking,' said my mother with seeming irrelevance, 'we were up on Constitution Hill and Daddie caught his walking stick in the loop of my sash!' The aunties' laughter that greeted this reminiscence seemed to us unaccountable! However, we joined in merrily enough, glad to express our joy of heart.

We always made for the monkeys, parrots, and peacocks to be seen by the fresh-water lake. One parrot would always answer 'Four o'clock', if asked the time – a miracle of intelligence we felt, quite in keeping with the wonder of our surroundings.

We always took a bag of pieces for the swans. We approached them with an odd mixture of fear and fascination. A train would pass; its whole length visible, like a toy, as it crossed the lake. We gazed across the sparkling water to Sandbanks, Brownsea Island and the Purbeck Hills, thinking of summers past and future.

The turkey and ourselves arrived back together at Grandma's house. An obliging local baker heated his oven and accomplished great things in the way of basting for some of his customers while the accessories to our Christmas dinner were cooked at home. It seemed to me that the turkey was quite two feet high as it obscured my view of the relative opposite me. The reason must have been that my own chin was so near the table in those days.

For years the family tabby cat sat on a chair, her front paws neatly placed together on the extreme edge of the table. She behaved perfectly throughout the first course but the moment the plates were cleared she ran to the kitchen ignoring all invitations to sit up and see the Christmas pudding come in.

After dinner we were made to rest, always objecting but finally sleeping soundly and having to be roused for tea.

Now we were dressed in our best. Other members of the family arrived after tea. Grandpa and Grandma sat each side of the fireplace, king and queen. And now the fun began. Family Coach, Stations, Musical Chairs, Hunt the Thimble, till everybody was glad to rest.

Then the children were called upon to recite. I remember regaling the audience with a poem beginning:

> A fair little girl sat under a tree
> Sewing as long as her eyes could see,
> Then folded her work and laid it right
> And said, 'Dear work, goodnight, goodnight'!

At last weariness began to descend upon us. Grandfather lifted down his Bible. A gentle hush fell over the gathering. Youngest ones were lifted on to laps. Every year Grandfather read Psalm 103 to us all:

Bless the Lord, O my soul and forget not all His benefits.

The mercy of the Lord is free from everlasting to everlasting upon them that fear Him and His righteousness unto children's children.

We knelt reverently and listened as he mentioned us each by name, his own six children and their partners and each of us. How safe and secure and happy we felt as the uncles and aunties echoed his quiet 'Amen.'

Amidst an animated buzz of merry talk all kinds of plans were formed as the visitors put on their hats and coats.

'You are coming to our house tomorrow,' said the eldest auntie who lived in Wimborne road. We beamed at her, delighted at the prospect.

Those who lived elsewhere in Poole, Parkstone and Hamworthy, were now ready to start, while we, privileged beyond the ordinary, stayed under the home roof echoing in our dreams the age old music of the Psalms. 'Bless the Lord, O, my soul. Bless the Lord, O my soul.'

To Make a Rich Plum Cake
By Mrs Walmsley, 1780

✳

1lb of butter well pressed and worked, add 1lb pounded loaf sugar.
Then add 12 eggs yolks and 8 whites of eggs,
1lb Flour,
3lb Currants,
½lb. blanched almonds,
½ pint brandy.
The almonds to be steeped overnight in the brandy.
Put one part of the mixture into a hoop and cover the top thickly
with sliced candied peel, mixed thus:
¼lb. Citron peel,
½lb Orange peel,
6ozs Lemon peel.
Put the rest of the mixture into the hoop on top of the peel.
Bake two hours in a slow oven.
Then put on top an icing of pounded sugar, almonds, and the
whites of eggs. Bake half an hour.

A Christmas Frolic

From the Dorset County Chronicle, *December 1829*

✳

The Christmas edition of the Dorset County Chronicle *in 1829 reported an affray caused by the Christmas celebrations of 'a party of soldiers drinking in The Three Mariners public house' in Dorchester with a party of townsmen from the Fordington area (which Thomas Hardy described as 'the mildewed leaf in the flourishing Casterbridge plant' in his Dorchester novel* The Mayor of Casterbridge*). This sixteenth-century tavern in the High Street was also celebrated by Thomas Hardy in his novel as the inn where Donald Farfrae stays on his arrival in Dorchester and where he makes such an impact on the locals and on his future wife, Elizabeth Jane, by his spirited and emotional singing of Scottish songs in the bar. Sadly the building was destroyed in the nineteenth century, all but a Tudor arch which still survives on the street front. The barracks were part of the castle complex at the western end of town.*

A dispute having arisen on some trivial topic, words soon gave way to blows, and the soldiers, drawing their swords, attacked the townsmen without distinction, and wounded several very seriously. The others procured spits, pokers, pitchforks, or any other weapon they could lay their hands on, and a general melee ensued. The soldiers retreated up the High Street towards the barracks, cutting at everyone in their progress, and pelted by the populace with stones etc.

Above: Victorian Dorchester.

Left: The surviving Tudor arch of the Three Mariners Inn in High East Street, Dorchester (photograph by Geoff Doel).

The Great Minterne Run, 19 December 1849

By Henry Symonds (1817-1895)

From Runs & Sporting Notes from Dorsetshire
(Blandford: Edward Derham, 1899)

'The best hunt ever known in Dorsetshire' is how Henry Symonds described the Minterne Hunt, which took place in midwinter 1849.

December 19th, 1849. – Met at Upcerne Wood, where they found immediately, going away directly for Batcombe, where the fox was lost. Found again at Minterne, – a brace – one of which the hounds killed. Treadwell caught a glimpse of the other fox, which looked like a

traveller; neither was he mistaken. The hounds being clapped on his line, he went away directly through Upcerne for Sydling Wood, turned to the left across the meadows, and up the hill for Cerne Park, but leaving it a little on the left, he dashed away across the Cerne road to Nether Cerne, where the wind being puffed out of him by the pace he had to go by Jem and his rattlers, he lay down in a pit; here Jem thought to nab him, when he jumped up in full view. By this short respite, having obtained second wind, he showed his agility by out-running his pursuers and turning back through Upcerne Park, went over the hills to Upcerne Wood. Again, not fancying the pace (he had been pressed through it before) he turned away to the right, down the hill, going straight by the Cerne Union House, across the enclosures by the town, away over the Godmanston and Grimston Downs, and through the Madjeston watermeadows, where divers casualties occurred from heavy work and blown horses, and the majority of the horsemen wishing he would never top the hill; but this sturdy old customer was not to be handled yet, for over the hill he went, as fresh as a four-year-old, through Frampton plantations, and crossing the Dorchester turnpike, dashed into the Frampton water-meadows and across the river, setting his head straight over the hill for the plantations and arable fields beyond, where some stuck fast and others were reduced to a trot, then to East Compton. 'Ah,' said Jem, 'we shall have you here by boy,' but as if divining Jem's wicked intentions, he suddenly changed his route, and turned up across the Compton ewe-leazes, and the old Roman road, down to Winterborne village. Here, all who remained with the hounds earnestly wished this long-winded varmint might take refuge in some barn or outhouse, and save their horses further exertions; and a little check near the village induced Jem to entertain the belief that his enemy's career was coming to a close (he was feeling for his pocket-knife to 'brush' him) when 'Barmaid' hit off the scent again to the right, across the Dorchester and Bridport road, and away went the pack again, thro' Winterborne plantations, straight over the downs for Whatcombe earths, but, disdaining these, our gallant fox held on his course by Kingston Russell House, across the water-meadows, as if for Foxholes Covert, which, however he left to the right and went up the hill by Winterborne long plantations, and bearing to the right again by the keeper's house, made for the laurels in Mr Williams' pleasure grounds at Bridehead House, where he was killed, after the best run ever known in Dorsetshire. The distance from point to point was about 15 miles, and the ground traversed by the hounds not less than 25 miles; done in two hours and a fraction. There was a cold sleet and snow falling all the time, and a piercing freezing wind.

'Ben' Jennings, a Dorset Huntsman, 1835.

Keepen Up O' Christmas
By William Barnes

✳

Another rich and vital Christmas offering from Barnes' seasonal collection of dialect poems. Udal says that 'forfeits was a very favourite amusement with Dorset folk during the long winter evenings, and more particularly at Christmas-tide, when the family circle had generally more than its usual complement.

There are many different versions of the game of forfeit in Dorset tradition. Barnes describes one called 'Snappen tongs' in his Glossary of the Dorset Dialect (1863), in which players stand up and one seat is removed and when the tongs are snapped, the one who fails to get a seat pays a forfeit.

An' zoo you didden come athirt,
To have zome fun last night: how wer't?
Vor we'd a-worked wi' all our might
To scour the iron things up bright,
An' brush'd an' scrubb'd the house all drough;
An' brought in vor a brand, a plock
O' wood so big's an uppen-stock
An' hung a bough o' misseltoo,
An' ax'd a merry friend or two,
To keepen up o' Christmas.

An' there wer wold an' young; an' Bill,
Soon after dark, stalk'd up vrom mill.
An' when he wer a-comin near,

Forfeits, a favourite
Victorian game.

He whissled loud vor me to hear;
Then roun' my head my frock I roll'd,
An' stood on orcha'd like a post,
To meake en think I wer a ghost.
But he wer up to't, an did scwold
To vind me stannen in the cwold,
A-keepen up o' Christmas.

We play'd at Forfeits, an' we spun
The trencher roun', an' meade such fun!
An' had a geame o' dree-ceard loo,
An' then begun to hunt the shoe.
An' all the wold vo'k zitten near,
A-chatten roun' the vier pleace,
Did smile in woone another's feace,
An' sheake right hands wi' hearty cheer,
An' let their left hands spill their beer,
A-keepen up o' Christmas.

The Christmas Piece
By Charles Mayo and John Short

In the 1830s education was neither obligatory nor free. The better-off working classes and lower middle classes sent their children to Day Schools often set up by Christian philanthropists but run by religious bodies and where a weekly fee was charged. This effectively excluded the children of the poorest section of Dorset society, who had to seek their education in the free Sunday schools. Day School boys and girls were given Christmas Pieces (often a broadsheet or religious tract) to copy and take home to their parents at Christmastime – these were the forerunners of the Christmas card. Printed below are two short articles on 'The Christmas Piece' from Somerset and Dorset Notes and Queries; *the first was written in 1899 by the Dorset editor of the magazine from 1888-1921, Charles Mayo, and the second is a follow-up by John Short from a subsequent issue.*

'The Christmas Piece' by Charles Mayo

The present season reminds me of what was a familiar object in my boyhood at this time of year. The 'Christmas Piece', as it was called, was a Broadsheet, measuring about twenty and a half inches, by sixteen and three quarters inches. (I take the dimensions from some specimens now before me) with a blank space in the midst round which was a border of rude engravings, still more rudely painted by hand in gaudy colours, representing a set of subjects from the Bible or a series of historical scenes derived from other sources. The story of Daniel was a favourite. The boys, who were the purchasers of these artistic productions, wrote

upon the blank space within the illustrated border, a specimen of their calligraphic skill, which might take the form of the Lord's Prayer, the Apostles' Creed, or some other short composition. The signature of the writer was also added. The 'Christmas Piece' was then complete, and was carried about shortly before Christmas, from house to house, in the form of a roll, with a view to extract a pecuniary reward from the admiring householder to whom it was exhibited at that open-hearted season. I remember this happening in the forties and fifties at Salisbury. Others may remember the same elsewhere. The same 'Piece' often did duty in several seasons.

I have before me some (unused) specimens, which were given me a few years ago by the son of the late Mr Penny, bookseller, Sherborne. They represent:

1. Christ the Good Shepherd
2. Balaam Blessing
3. The Life of Joseph
4. The Besieging of Jerusalem by Nebuchadnezzar
5. The Ten Commandments
6. The Crusaders. The Life of Richard the First
7. The Life of King Henry the Eighth
8. Queen Elizabeth

The arrangement is similar in all these broadsheets, viz., a long hand-coloured woodcut stretches across the top of the sheet and forms the most striking object in the 'Piece'. Six smaller engravings, also coloured, three on each side, form a right hand and left hand border; and the foot of the sheet is occupied with a long, more or less emblematic illustration, but on a much smaller scale than the head-piece.

The engravings are rude enough, and the colouring has only its brilliancy to recommend it. The head-piece of No. 3, representing the siege of Jerusalem by Nebuchadnezzar, is violently anachronistic, as several banners of the besiegers bear the S.P.Q.R.

'The Christmas Piece' by John Short

My recollection of these broadsheets goes back to 1830–1831. I remember writing two when about 9 years of age. One was, I think, the story of Daniel … The other was that of the disobedient Prophet, which

is very distinct in my mind because it gave me a great deal of trouble in writing the words exactly as they occur in 1 Kings, xiii, 28. We had to take our 'Pieces' home to show our progress in writing.

Absent-Mindedness in a Parish Choir

From 'A Few Crusted Characters' in Life's Little Ironies
by Thomas Hardy

✳

From the seventeenth to the nineteenth centuries, much church music in Dorset was played by quires of local musicians using a variety of string, woodwind and brass instruments to accompany boy singers. The local musicians composed music, and sometimes words, though in Dorset psalms were often used. This style of music is called West Gallery because of the special wooden galleries that were erected at the west end by the tower to accommodate the singers and musicians. A few of the galleries survive, notably at Puddletown and Worth Matravers; Stinsford Gallery has recently been rebuilt, but is dominated by the organ.

There are a number of revival West Gallery groups today, which show us how delightful the music is and causes us to question the Victorian 'aesthetic' judgement which swept these bands away, replacing them with barrel-organs, pianos, organs and harmoniums. Hardy lovingly describes the organisation of such quires in Under the Greenwood Tree, *and in its Preface:*

The zest of these bygone instrumentalists must have been keen and staying, to take them, as it did, on foot every Sunday, after a toilsome week through all weathers to the church, which often lay at a distance from their homes. They usually received so little in payment for their performances that their efforts were really a labour of love. In the parish I had in my mind when writing the present tale, the gratuities received yearly by the musicians at Christmas were somewhat as follows: From the manor-house ten shillings and a supper; from the vicar ten shillings; from the farmers five shillings each; from each cottage-household one shilling; amounting altogether to not more than ten shillings a head annually – just enough, as an old executant told me, to pay for their fiddle-strings, repairs, rosin, and music-paper (which they mostly ruled themselves). Their music in those days was all in their own manuscript, copied in the evenings after work, and their music-books were home bound.

This delightful story of the demise of the Longpuddle church quire shows the hazards of combining secular and sacred music, as of course the Hardy quire did with their country dance band where, as we see in Under the Greenwood Tree, *the band plays carols on Christmas night processing round the parish, then again at two church services on Christmas Day and then secular music (allowed after midnight by Old William) at the Christmas night party. They effectively had no sleep for two nights. On Christmas Day they are substandard after no sleep, which gives the zealous young vicar the chance to end their long association as church musicians and replace them with Fancy Day, whom he 'fancies'!*

The Longpuddle players (based on one of the villages in the Piddle Valley) have had a heavy time of it building up to Christmas and this combined with their efforts to overcome the cold in the church gallery, plus the length of the sermon, fatally undermines them. The story, as with the novel Under the Greenwood Tree, *dramatises the problems of the church quires in the early nineteenth century, when they were gradually eliminated from church music.*

The stories in Life's Little Ironies *are told by the occupants of a carrier van travelling from Casterbridge to Longpuddle, for the benefit of a fellow traveller who has returned after emigrating from Longpuddle thirty-five years earlier.*

It happened on Sunday after Christmas – the last Sunday ever they played in Longpuddle church gallery, as it turned out, though they didn't know it then. As you may know, sir, the players formed a very good band – almost as good as the Mellstock parish players that were led by the Dewys; and that's saying a great deal. There was Nicholas Puddingcome, the leader, with the first fiddle; there was Timothy Thomas, the bass-viol man; John Biles, the tenor fiddler, Dan'l Hornhead, with the serpent; Robert Dowdle, with the clarionet; and Mr Nicks, with the oboe – all sound and powerful musicians, and strong-winded men – they that blowed. For that reason they were very much in demand Christmas week for little reels and dancing parties; for they could turn a jig or a hornpipe out of hand as well as ever they could turn out a psalm, and perhaps better, not to speak irreverent. In short, one half-hour they could be playing a Christmas carol in the Squire's hall to the ladies and

Thomas Hardy's drawing of the Stinsford church west gallery and choir, based on a description by his father.

Yetminster parish church choir, drawn by Revd Looper, curate from 1831-1835.

gentlemen, and drinking tay and coffee with 'em as modest as saints; and the next, at The Tinker's Arms, blazing away like wild horses with the 'Dashing White Sergeant' to nine couple of dancers and more, and swallowing rum-and-cider hot as flame.

Well, this Christmas they'd been out to one rattling randy after another every night, and had got next to no sleep at all. Then came the Sunday after Christmas, their fatal day. 'Twas so mortal cold that year that they could hardly sit in the gallery; for though the congregation down in the body of the church had a stove to keep off the frost, the players in the gallery had nothing at all. So Nicholas said at morning service, when 'twas freezing an inch an hour, 'Please the Lord I won't stand this numbing weather no longer; this afternoon we'll have something in our insides to make us warm, if it cost a king's ransom.'

So he brought a gallon of hot brandy and beer, ready mixed, to church with him in the afternoon, and by keeping the jar well wrapped up in Timothy Thomas's bass-viol bag it kept drinkably warm till they wanted it, which was just a thimbleful in the Absolution, and another after the Creed, and the remainder at the beginning o' the sermon. When they'd had the last pull they felt quite comfortable and warm, and as the sermon went on – most unfortunately for 'em it was a long one that afternoon – they fell asleep, every man jack of 'em; and there they slept on as sound as rocks.

'Twas a very dark afternoon, and by the end of the sermon all you could see of the inside of the church were the pa'son's two candles alongside of him in the pulpit, and his spaking face behind 'em. The sermon being ended at last, the pa'son gie'd out the Evening Hymn. But no quire set about sounding up the tune, and the people began to turn their heads to learn the reason why, and then Levi Limpet, a boy who sat in the gallery, nudged Timothy and Nicholas, and said, 'Begin! Begin!'

'Hey? What?' says Nicholas, starting up; and the church being so dark and his head so muddled he thought he was at the party they had played at all the night before, and away he went, bow and fiddle, at 'The Devil among the Tailors', the favourite jig of our neighbourhood at that time. The rest of the band, being in same state of mind and nothing doubting, followed their leader with all their strength, according to custom. They poured out that there tune till the lower bass notes of 'The Devil among the Tailors' made the cobwebs in the roof shiver like ghosts; then Nicholas, seeing nobody moved, shouted out as he scraped (in his usual commanding way at dances when the folk didn't know the figures), 'Top couples cross hands! And when I make the fiddle squeak at the end, every man kiss his pardner under the mistletoe!'

The boy Levi was so frightened that he bolted down the gallery stairs and out homeward like lightning. The pa'son's hair fairly stood on end

Illustration to 'Absent-Mindedness in a Parish Choir' in *Harper's New Monthly Magazine*, 1891.

when he heard the evil tune raging through the church, and thinking the quire had gone crazy he held up his hand and: 'Stop, stop, stop! Stop, stop! What's this?' But they didn't hear'n for the noise of their own playing, and the more he called the louder they played.

Then the folks came out of their pews, wondering down to the ground, and saying; 'What do they mean by such wickedness! We shall be consumed like Sodom and Gomorrah!'

And the Squire, too, came out of his pew lined wi' green baize, where lots of lords and ladies visiting at the house were worshipping along with him, and went and stood in front of the gallery, and shook his fist in the musicians' faces, saying, 'What! In this reverent edifice! What!'

And at last they heard'n through their playing, and stopped.

'Never such an insulting, disgraceful thing – never!' Says the Squire, who couldn't rule his passion.

'Never!' says the pa'son, who had come down and stood beside him.

'Not if the Angels of Heaven,' says the Squire (he was a wickedish man, the Squire was, though now for once he happened to be on the Lord's side) – 'not if the Angels of Heaven come down,' he says, 'shall one of you villainous players ever sound a note in this church again; for the insult to me, and my family, and my visitors, and the pa'son, and God Almighty, that you've a-perpetrated this afternoon.

Then the unfortunate church band came to their senses, and remembered where they were; and 'twas a sight to see Nicholas Puddingcome and Timothy Thomas and John Biles creep down the gallery stairs with their fiddles under their arms, and poor Dan'l Hornhead with his serpent, and Robert Dowdle with his clarinet, all looking as little as ninepins; and out they went. The pa'son might have forgi'ed 'em when he learned the truth o't, but the Squire would not. That very week he sent for a barrel-organ that would play two-and-twenty new psalm-tunes, so exact and particular that, however sinful inclined you was, you could really play nothing but psalm-tunes whatsomever. He had a really respectable man to turn the winch, as I said, and the old players played no more.

The last traditional West Gallery quire was thought to be that of Winterbourne Abbas, which survived until 1940. The leader of the quire John Dunford, a thatcher, was photographed in 1897 at the age of seventy-two, having been playing in the quire for forty-two years. He played the clarinet and his son (who continued with the quire until its demise) the bass viol; there was also a clarinet in the Winterbourne Quire. The Hardy quire at Stinsford was entirely strings.

Many West Gallery hymns survive; there are the Hardy family manuscripts and

surviving manuscripts from Puddletown, Combe Keynes and Bloxworth. Somerset and Dorset Notes and Queries *printed a whole selection from the 'Christmas carol-singers at Long Burton', which had been in their repertory for some time; one of them was thought to have been brought to the village by a hay-trusser from Upwey. Carols about the shepherds were favourites in the sheep-farming county of Dorset.*

John Dunford, thatcher, parish clerk and leader of the West Gallery Quire in Winterbourne Abbas, with his clarinet, 1897.

'While Shepherds Were Feeding Their Flocks in the Field'

The Christmas Kissing Bough
By Laurence Whistler

✳

Last Christmas there began to be revived in a number of English homes a very English and delightful Christmas custom. Candlelit kissing boughs began to hang from ceilings again – as they used to hang before the German Christmas tree replaced them. Nobody wants to replace the Christmas tree; but there are certainly many who would make a kissing bough if they saw one.

I have not the space here, to tell the whole story of this charming device, but I will explain the construction of it. The kissing bough takes the shape of a globe or a crown, and the framework can be made at home out of pliable wire, and will then last through any number of Christmases. For the globe, five separate circles of wire are first formed, all exactly alike, and perhaps two feet across. One of these will become the 'equator' and the other four will be evenly spaced around it to form

A Christmas garland.

eight 'meridians'. These are then bound at the 'equator' and the 'poles' with a very fine binding wire, and the framework is then complete. It must now be covered entirely with long strips of evergreen, bound on with the same fine wire. The kissing bough is shapely and formal – not fussy or untidy; therefore a small leafed evergreen should be used, preferably box.

Eight coloured candles are now clipped or wired to the 'equator' and another can form a circle lower down, about three inches in radius from the 'south pole.' In the centre of all hang seven bright red apples, each one tied by the stalk to a coloured ribbon, which itself is tied with a bow to the 'north pole'. But if the stalks have gone, the ribbon can be threaded through the core with a bodkin and knotted at the end. Improvisation has always been liked; and in a dearth of red apples, green have been used – or oranges – or even a silver or golden ball, and this last will reflect the flames of the candle all round it.

The globe is now hung on wire or red braid from a strong hood in the ceiling; and then, finally, a bunch of mistletoe is tied to the bottom – to earn the kissing bough its name (though in the north it has often been made without it). Here the young couples met for a laughing embrace, here carols were sung, and here were exchanged the last kisses on Christmas Eve.

For a very low room the crown is more appropriate. It resembles the globe in construction, except that the 'meridians' short stop at the 'equator', with one red apple below each, and the mistletoe hangs in the centre.

[...] the reader must picture to himself how different it is to enter a room lit by these buoyant flames and to look upon the glowing apples and leaves – at the very symbol and crown of a Christmas in England, the Christmas kissing bough.

The Beginning of the
Postal Traffic in Swanage
By William Masters Hardy

✳

The collection, dispatch and delivery of mail has always been an important part of the work of the Post Office and Hardy's valuable account shows how the service was developed in Swanage from the late eighteenth century into the Edwardian period.

Hardy makes mention of the mail coach system, which was begun in 1784 by John Palmer and ran efficiently for fifty years (though winter weather tended to disrupt the service). Mail coaches were usually drawn by four horses and could travel at a speed of twelve miles an hour on a good road. Where roads were difficult or rivers had to be forded, two trace horses were added. Highwaymen being a threat at this period, an armed guard escort was always on board to guard the mail. Hardy also mentions the turnpike roads with their tollgates and tollhouses. Tolls collected were used for the repair and maintenance of the roads.

I may here incidentally mention what progress has been made in Swanage in respect to the postal traffic, which has grown from a small beginning to a considerable volume. In the latter part of the 18th Century my great grandfather, Jos. Rawles, lived in High Street, on the top of Church Hill, on the site of the present infant school. He had been a soldier, and had fought in the Continental wars, and was wounded, invalided home, and received a small pension. He afterwards obtained the appointment of postman, and had to carry the mail bags from

The mail coach ploughing its way through a snowdrift, from W. Outram Tristram's *Coaching Days and Coaching Ways* (1894).

Swanage to Wareham by way of Kingston and Corfe Castle, starting on Mondays, sleeping at Wareham, and returning on Tuesdays, delivering and collecting letters and papers *en route*. In addition to his mail bags he carried a brace of loaded pistols for self-defence, should he be waylaid on his lonely journey. The number of letters and papers daily then on an average was about 25. He has trudged to Wareham and back three times weekly, resting on the Sabbath day. The postage then amounted to 6d. or 8d., according to the distance, eightpence being charged for letters to Scotland. In 1800 the postman was allowed a horse to ride, and he was thus enabled to go and return daily. Later on, in the Twenties, was instituted a covered mail cart, which carried passengers, in addition to the mail bags, and it proved a great boon to many who were too poor to hire a special conveyance to visit their distant friends in case of necessity or on a holiday. The mail man at this date was named William Masters. In 1848 the letters and papers averaged about 30 a day. In 1850 a mail coach was established in addition to the mail cart. It left Swanage at nine in the morning and returned from Wareham in the afternoon, arriving at Swanage about three o'clock. The coach proprietor was named Wignall, and the conductor Essex. I remember very well meeting an old postman named James Manwell delivering the letters, holding them all in his left hand, arranged for delivery, as he went on his round. This old man resided at Herston, and looked after the turnpike gate, and thus naturally retained the Herston letters till he returned there to dinner. After Mr Wignall ceased running the coach, the mails were brought by coach and four from the Red Lion, Wareham, until the advent of the railway, which now brings the mails; but the old style of collecting letters &c., by mail cart from Herston, Langton, Kingston, and Corfe Castle is still in vogue. As a contrast to the size of the mail mentioned at the beginning of this paragraph, the number of letters, packets, parcels, &c., delivered in the Swanage town district at the beginning of the 20th Century was on an average 21,294 weekly, and there was a staff of 16 officials. And towards the end of February, 1908, a fine new Post Office, built by Messrs. Parsons and Haytor, in Station Road, was opened to the public, affording ampler accommodation for the various branches of the postal business than the old office in the High Street.

Waiting for the mail coach on Christmas Eve, from *Coaching Days and Coaching Ways*.

A Christmas Ghost Story
By Thomas Hardy

This poem about the Boer War (which Hardy opposed) was published in the
Westminster Gazette *on 23 December 1899 and later in Hardy's* Poems of
the Past and the Present *in 1901. Hardy liked to publish poems associated
with Christmas Eve and he appended the words 'Christmas-eve 1899' to the
poem.*

South of the Line, inland from far Durban
A mouldering soldier lies – your countryman.
Awry and doubled up are his gray bones,
And on the breeze his puzzled phantom moans
Nightly to clear Canopus: 'I would know
By whom and when the All-Earth-gladding Law
Of Peace, brought in by that Man Crucified,
Was ruled to be inept, and set aside?
And what of logic or of truth appears
In tacking 'Anno Domini' to the years?
Near twenty-hundred liveried thus have hied,
But tarries yet the Cause for which He died.'

A Christmas Sermon Against Looting from Wrecked Ships

By Thomas Francklyn, Rector of Langton Herring and Vicar of Fleet

There was a long coastal tradition in Dorset of risking life to save shipwrecked mariners. Unfortunately this went hand-in-hand with seizing shipwrecked articles, which the local communities treated as customary right. The Isle of Portland and its associated Chesil Beach, which linked it to the mainland near to West Bay, were notorious areas for shipwrecks. On Christmas Day 1600 it is recorded that more than twenty ships were wrecked off Chesil Beach, including the privateer Isobel *and the Spanish ship she had been pursuing. Traditions of deliberately wrecking ships and hazarding life (fostered by Daphne Du Maurier's romantic Cornish treatment in* Jamaica Inn*) may have certainly been exaggerated as regards Dorset at least, but there are numerous accounts of looting wrecked ships in the area. For example, in January 1762, the French privateer* Zenobie *was wrecked on Chesil Beach; the seventy-one survivors were robbed and stripped and their clothes taken. George III was so enraged when he learnt of their mistreatment that he ordered the victims to be sent back to France, rather than be kept as prisoners, even though Britain and France were at war at the time. The* London Journal *of 1752 reported that 'all the people of Abbotsbury, including the Vicar, are thieves, smugglers and plunderers of wrecks'.*

The local clergy, while sensitive to the bravery of their congregations in saving life, were uneasy about the moral implications of wrecking. Eventually Thomas Francklyn, the rector of Langton Herring and vicar of Fleet (both parishes facing

Portland across the Chesil) preached a sermon on 22 December 1754 at Fleet and Chickerel, attacking the practice of looting from wrecked ships on the Chesil. This made such an impact locally that it was later published as a pamphlet, extracts of which are printed below.

The recent Act of Parliament to which Francklyn refers supplements one from the twelfth year of the reign of Queen Anne; he prints extracts from both in his pamphlet. The earlier act directs those in authority that they shall 'upon Application made by the Commander of any Ship in Distress or Stranded, and run Ashore, summon as many Men as shall be thought necessary to preserve the Ship and Cargo' for which the men can be rewarded by payment. The Act then goes specifically to say that:

If any Person beside those empowered to act in saving the said Ship and Cargo, shall Endeavour to enter on Board such Ship in Distress or stranded, without Leave of the Master of the Ship, or Person empowered to employ Men to save it, or shall molest or hinder any of them that are

A shipwreck near
Worbarrow Bay.

saving it, or when Goods are saved shall take out the Marks, or deface them, before they are taken down in a Book provided by the Master and Officer of Customs, in twenty Days, shall make double Satisfaction to the Party grieved, at the Discretion of the two next Justices of the Peace, or be sent to hard Labour at the House of Correction for twelve Months; and any such Master or Officer of Customs may repel by Force any such Person who will enter or press Aboard such Ship in Distress without Leave or Consent, and molest them in preserving the Ship or Cargo.

Even more specifically, the 'recent' Act of the twenty-sixth year of the reign of George II provides that:

To plunder Ships in Distress, or steal, take away, or destroy any of their Materials or Goods when stranded, wreck'd or lost, or hinder Men from escaping the Danger of the Sea, or to put out false Lights to bring them into Danger, is Felony without their Clergy.

Serious Advice and Fair Warning To all that live upon the Sea-Coast of England and Wales, particularly to those in the Neighbourhood of Weymouth and Portland.
By Thomas Francklyn

To see those, who, from a Sense of the like Dangers and Sufferings, should, one would think, be always ready to assist their Brethren, in saving the small Remains of a broken Voyage, rob them of the few Clothes and that little Venture which a poor, half-drowned Sailor had saved out of the Water, at the Peril of his Life, to refresh him when ashore, and to cover his naked Family, that has liv'd on the Credit of his Wages, which, perhaps, are lost with the Ship, is enough to make the Stones upon the Shore cry out, if Men were silent; and he that can be an indifferent Spectator of a Shipwreck attended with such like Circumstances, as too often happen, must be entirely void of Religion and Humanity; a Stranger to every other Use of Law, and Justice, and Compassion, than to break thro' them all, when they oppose his Appetite for Plunder.

It has been my Lot to have lived many Years in such a Situation, as to have been an Eye-Witness of several Shipwrecks, and after repeated Expostulations with many of my Neighbours, in order to revive in them the natural Sentiments of Humanity, and stir up the Principles of Benevolence and Compassion, as well as Honesty, in their Hearts, I thought it my Duty to warn them from the Pulpit, to forsake a Practice which was become habitual, and almost general, and therefore looked upon as right and lawful by most of them, till the late penal Law shew'd them it was illegal, and that the Offenders would be severely punished

And being sensible that the Act of Parliament was not calculated only for this Neighbourhood, but that the same Spirit reigns along the Coast, I resolved to make it as useful, by making it as general as possible. And I hope the well-disposed Gentry will promote the Design, by dispersing the Sermon among their Neighbours and Tenants on the Sea-Coast, to try what may be done towards stopping the Progress of an Evil generally complained of, and justly styled in the Act itself, 'An Enormity that is a Scandal to the Nation'.

As my Audience consisted chiefly of little Farmers and Fishermen, I was obliged to adapt my Discourse to their Capacity; and this, I presume, is the common Standard of all concerned in this Advice. And if we can reclaim the Poor, instruct the Ignorant, and make them keep at Home, and forbear plundering, it is to be hoped the other Farmers and better Sort of People will not venture; and surely they ought to be ashamed to send their Servants and Teams upon the Strand, to steal and carry off other Mens' Property. Men who have Nothing will sometimes turn Thieves; but they who have Property of their own, should not set an Example that may encourage others to rob them.

A Sermon Preached at Fleet and Chickerel on the twenty-second of December, 1754. On Occasion of several Ships being at that Time stranded on the Coast.
Acts xxviii. 1. 2-10v:

And when we were escaped then we knew that the Island was called Melita.

And the barborous People shewed us no little Kindness. For they kindled a Fire and received us every one, because of the present Rain and because of the Cold:

And when we departed they laded us with such Things as were necessary.

In these Words the sacred Historian gratefully records the humane Treatment St. Paul and his Companions met with after their providential Escape from the Dangers of the Sea... The Voice of Nature and of Grace cries out in Behalf of Mercy, and he that can behold others Misery without a compassionate Sense of it, is so far from being of a Christian Temper, that he is less than Man; has lost all that is tender and merciful in Human Nature... To do all Men Justice, I must own, that I know no

All Saints church in
Wyke and the Isle
of Portland. Etching
from T.H. Williams'
*A Walk on the Coast of
Dorsetshire from Lyme
to Lulworth.*

one in this Neighbourhood that is not industrious on all Occasions to save the Lives of them that are cast on Shore. But there is a Practice that is of too near an Affinity to it, from which very few in the Compass of my Acquaintance in these Parts can fairly be acquitted; and it has a long Time almost universally prevailed along the Sea-Coast, though it be universally detested and complained of by every thinking Man, and that is, plundering the Ships that are stranded of that which might be saved for the Merchants and Owners.

This has long been looked upon as a Thing right and lawful to be done by them who received it from their Forefathers, and practised it betimes. And indeed, nothing can reconcile an Act so vile, so sordid and so shocking to any one's Reason or Conscience, but the Frequency of committing it.

Use and Custom can alone so alter the Appearance, though not the Nature of Things, as to make some Men call Evil Good, and Good Evil. Custom and Practice they foolishly imagine to be capable of giving them a Right and Title to whatever they can pillage from a

Shipwreck, though it is expressly contrary to Reason and Religion, and the common Sense of Mankind. It is unhappily true that Custom does encourage though it cannot excuse Men in doing what is wrong. Example is a powerful Thing, and it were greatly to be wished that the Examples for public Worship, Virtue, Goodness, Seriousness, and every Quality to Society, were more numerous among all Ranks of Men than it is to be feared they are.

We can't well suppose the barbarous People in the Text to have reasoned in the Manner some Men now do; for they not only supported and entertained that numerous Company while they waited for a Passage into Italy, but when they departed they laded them with such Things as were necessary for their Voyage.

These ignorant but honest People knew no Right they had to enrich themselves by other Mens Misfortunes, but thought themselves obliged to assist and provide for them. And to put them in a Capacity to retrieve what they had lost.

St Aldhelm's Head, scene of many shipwrecks. The monks of Sherborne set up a chapel on the headland and a beacon for sailors.

77

Peter of Pomfret, AD 1212
By W. Winslow

*

This highly imaginative construct of the events leading to the arrest and death of the saintly Peter of Pomfret on New Year's Night 1212 was written for the Bournemouth Literature and Art Group by a Dr W. Winslow, a local physician practising in Bournemouth in 1914. Corfe Castle, the scene of Peter's incarceration in iron chains, had a suitably grisly reputation and provided the perfect backdrop for such a gothic tale. King John has acquired such an evil reputation historically that few would question this delightful 'music-hall villain' presentation here as a cruel and treacherous monarch with a 'snarling moody cackle', forever 'hissing' and stroking of 'his cruel, blond fringed lips'. Ironically, modern scholarship seems to suggest that the king was cultured and politically astute while Peter the Hermit may have been a near insane fanatic.

I High in his castle keep at Corfe,
   The night of the New Year,
   King John was feasting wantonly
   But in his heart was fear

   He leaned his elbow on the board,
   And, restlessly his hand
   Now swept aside his shaggy mane,
   Now gestured a command,

Now tugged his tawny, square-hewn beard,
Now hid his hooded lips,
Now cast across his wild, blue eyes
An ominous eclipse.

For, glaring hard on lout and lord,
For each he strove to wring
An answer to the gnawing doubt,
'Art loyal to thy king ?'

To guard his treasure too; to ward
His captives: then a-chafe,
He muttered, as he panted hard,
'Here — here — I must be safe !'

Sudden, within the banquet hall,
A hubbub hoarse arose,
Quelled by a clarion monotone
Which chanted to a close;

And then such plaudits rent the air,
Such savagery of joy,
That on his seneschal the king
Glared questionful annoy.

The white-haired seneschal drew nigh,
And bent a quaking knee :
'Sire, 'tis a madman monk who stirs
Thy varlets to such glee.'

'A madman monk!' The monarch growled,
'Ha! Fetch him for our mirth.'
The seneschal grew pale, 'Great lord,
The knave is nothing worth.'

'Have I not spoken?' Snarled the king,
The greybeard grovelled low;
'Nay, good my lord, do not this thing,
And bid the madman go.'

The moody king laughed evilly:
'My jester's japes grow thin.
Shall we not share our varlet's glee?
Go: fetch they madman in.'

The greybeard wailed, 'My liege, be warned –'
'Obey! Begone!' He fled,
And on the crowded hall there fell
Silence as of the dead.

II   Combing his cruel, blond fringed lips,
The monarch eyed the door;
It opened, and a figure frail
Strode lightly up the floor.

His puny form, his pallid face,
His comely, high-poised head,
Candled two coal-black, flaming eyes
That strook the throng with dread.

'Ha, John!' he cried, 'Thou doest well
My summons to obey.'
'Thy summons?' Gasped the startled king,
'Some demon art thou?' 'Nay –

Peter of Pomfret men me call.'
'Then, Peter, have a care.
Thou'rt speaking to thy king.' 'False John,
'Tis thou that must beware.

I voice, this night, the will of One
Who reigns the King of kings.
Down on thy knees, thou sin-stained man!'
The monarch twirled his rings,

And laughed full fiendishly. 'Mad monk,
If I but give the word
Thy blasphemous tongue shall be out-torn.'
The flame-black eyes ne'er stirred.

But burnt their gaze into John's soul.
'Sinner,' he cried, 'the tale
Of thy transgressions who can tell?
One tongue may ill avail.

E'en at this moment thou dost hold,
Within these blood-soaked walls,
Princesses three in durance vile;
Two dozen knights, thy thralls.

Pent in a foul, black, airless pit,
Below thy Dungeon Tower,
Thou startest – John the table smote:
'Thou too shall feel my power.

There shalt thou also starve.' The monk
Flung high his shaven face;
'I would to God this carcase vile
Might suffer in their place!

But now, alas! That may not be
Know, John (his eyes grew dim),
Already two-and-twenty-knights
Lie dead within that grim

Polluted pit. Be merciful.
Spare the surviving twain!
'Not I!' The monarch roared, and tossed
Abroad his tawny mane.

'Bethink thee,' pled the monk, 'ere long
Thyself for rue may cry –'
'This passeth patience!' stormed the king,
'Mad croaker, thou shalt die !'

Peter of Pomfret, with two strides,
Flamed at the tyrant's knee;
The coward quailed beneath his gaze,
And turned as though to flee.

But loud the clarion voice rang forth,
'John, thou hast cast away
Thy one last hope of pardon. Now
No man thy doom can stay.

Before this year is out, thy crown,
False monarch, thou shalt lose –
'Ah,' breathed the listening courtier-crowd,
Transported at the news.

'Seize him!' The tyrant yelled. Now stirred.
The clarion rang, 'Nay, hear!
I tell you, lords, this tyrant foul
In less than half a year,

Shall lowly lout, and homage pay
To one who reigns o'er kings –'
'Will no one strike the madman dead?'
Howled John. But mutterings.

Ran lightning-like throughout the throng,
And no one moved. Again
The clarion voice rang forth, 'False John,
But three years hence thou'lt drain

Thy death-draught –' 'Traitor! Liar! – Lords,
Butcher the cur!' Screamed John.
Peter of Pomfret meekly turned,
His orbs no longer shone:

With up-turned palms he faced the crowd:
'Take me! My say is said,
Passed just mine hour of might: and now
My lot lies with the dead.'

'Stab him!' Hissed John. The ashen monk
Threading the festal boards
With head abased, crept gropingly
Toward the bristling swords.

'Stay, speedy death were doom too kind,'
Blared John, 'Let him be bound,
And, at my fleetest courser's heels,
Be clattered o'er the ground;

Then high let him be hanged, that all
May see, with shuddering,
How traitors fare who madly dare
To flout their lord and king.'

III   Snuff-eyed and pithless drooped the monk,
Deaf to the mob's appears,
A mettled courser's heels.

They galloped their palpitant living sledge
To Warehamand back again;
Then hanged on high the gore-grimed bones
In a rusted iron chain.

Oft stayed the vengeful king to taunt
The putrid, blackening mass:
'Now Peter, which of us can vaunt?
Whose words have come to pass?'

Yet, ere three months had fled, King John
At Pandulf's foot abased,
Had yielded up his crown to Rome,
World-scorned and self-disgraced.

Then, three years later, while in flight,
Deserted and defied
At Swineshead, maugre fever-blight,
In wild debauchery, one night,
Fell poison unawares he plight,
And horribly he died.

Corfe Castle, from
an early *Guide to
Corfe Castle*.

The Dorsets in the Great War

By Sir Frederick Treves

From the Dorset Year Books *1915-16 and 1918-19*

✳

Sir Frederick Treves (1853-1923) was the royal surgeon to Edward VII and editor of the Dorset Year Book *for many years. Treves was a fervent patriot and deeply attached to his beloved Dorset. The following two pieces which he wrote for the 1915-16 and 1918-19 Christmas editions of the journal differ markedly in mood. 'What the Dorsets have Done in the Great War' (1915) sketches the progress of the Dorset battalions in theatres of war in Europe, the Near East and India and reflects Treves' strongly held view that the Dorsets are heroically employed and their sacrifice is noble. The second piece, 'A Draft of the Dorsets' (1918) , is sombre and despairing. The battles of Marne, Ypres, the Somme and Passchendaele have all been fought with the most terrible slaughter on either side. Now there is widespread criticism at home of the military commanders while the men are known to be enduring the most appalling hardships. The patriotic young Dorset men observed by Treves on Christmas Eve 1918 and who are answering England's call to arms, he suggests, are marching to their death.*

What the Dorsets Have Done in The Great War

If you chance to glance down a casualty list – any one will do – you will in all probability find the Dorsets in it somewhere. If the mention is not from Flanders, it is from the Dardanelles or Persia. But there you will find your Dorset man who has yielded up his life or taken his wound in the interests of the country. It is a great story, this story of Dorset and the War, but not until the campaign is at an end shall we know what Dorset has really done. Up till now we have had to content ourselves with the stories that come home, stories of great bravery and fearful losses, but always stories that make us proud that we come from Dorset, where they breed such men as these heroes are made of.

It is not easy to get together a connected movement of the Dorset battalions in the war. We know that the 1st Battalion went out to Flanders with the Expeditionary Force in the first days of the war, that the 2nd Battalion went to the Persian Gulf, that the 3rd are at Wyke, from whence they made good the losses of the of the 1st and 2nd Battalions, that the 4th (Territorial) Dorsets with the Dorset Battery of Artillery are in India, the 5th Dorsets in the Dardanelles, and the 6th and youngest Battalion is in Flanders. We know, too, that the Dorset Yeomanry was grievously cut up in the spring of this year in Gallipoli.

The Dorsets in Flanders, from the *Dorset Year Book*, 1915–16.

All this we know. But some day, when the stress and turmoil of this war has burnt itself out, and details of what these battalions have been through are accessible, some man of Dorset will sit himself down and write a history of the Dorsets and the Great War, a history which will make his fellow men of the soil say when they read it: 'I am thankful that, by the grace of God, I am a man of Dorset'.

A Draft of the Dorsets

December 24th. 'A draft of the Dorsets left for the Front this morning.'
– Local Paper

It was a winter of despair, grey, shuddering and dark. For weary days there had been no change: no wind had blown; no sun had shone. A clammy mist buried alive the little town and shut it off from the world. Somewhere beyond the mist were the downs and the sea and white roads leading to neighbourly towns; but all touch with these things was lost. The place was imprisoned in a cell of cloud.

There are winters when a clear wind rings across the hills like a sound of a bell, when the sky is blue and the sun glitters on the ice as on a sheet of agate, and when:

Deep on the courent roofs the snows
Are sparkling to the moon;

But here it seemed to be neither winter, nor autumn, nor spring. It was, moreover, twilight the whole day through. Sunrise and sunset have ceased to be, and the time may already have come, of which the learned speak, when the sun shall die out of the heavens. In the summer, in days of peace, there was no brighter little town that this, full of laughter and merriment, but now, in the winter of war, it had become dumb, stupefied and blind.

There was a depot of the Dorset Regiment in the place, and now and then drafts were sent off to the Front. They left early in the morning about 8 a.m. I saw one draft go by on Christmas Eve. I never saw a second one. Others I heard go by, as I lay in bed, but I could not get up to look at them, for the sight was too pitiable.

The hotel in which I stayed was on the sea road, between the depot and the railway station. Each draft, however small, was conducted to the station by the band of the regiment and passed beneath the hotel windows. On this Christmas Eve I heard in the distance the sound of a military band. It was evidently approaching. I jumped out of bed in the dark and threw open the old-fashioned shutters. It was barely light – a dismal, unkindly dawn. The warmth of the room contrasted with the damp and shivering world outside. The sullen mist was over all. Trickles of moisture crossed the black, asphalt road like snail tracks on coal. There was not a living thing in sight. But for its rows of seats and the chilled shrubs that formed the ghost of a garden border the promenade was deserted. From a wet board hung skin-like shreds of paper announcing a concert held three years ago. A signpost pointed to 'The Tennis Courts', while out of the fog on the beach rose the frivolous roof of the bathing saloon surmounted by a tattered flag. The sea was invisible, but the muffled sound of languid waves could just be heard – a sound as monotonous as a funeral bell.

The music of the band drew nearer and then there became audible the solemn, measured tread of marching men. To these ordered and mechanical sounds the irregular murmur of the unseen sea was as the voice of eternity. The band was playing a jaunty music-hall air, so incongruous as to be horrible. The bandsmen played it ill, as if they felt the heartlessness of the merry tune.

The men of the draft who tramped behind were few in number, some twenty in all. They were as fully equipped as if they were marching up to the front line. There were more bundles than men, so that the company seemed almost buried under their packs, their haversacks, their bottles, their bandoliers, their entrenching tools and their rifles. They were well-nigh bent down by these many burdens. As it was Christmas Eve, each one might have been a terrifying Santa Claus laden with gifts that would carry death, misery and destruction to whomsoever they came upon.

They were off to the war. They marched gallantly enough, although their steps were little attune with the rollicking music of the band. A more fitting accompaniment was the tolling of the sea. Tomorrow would be Christmas Day, the cherished festival of the home which is never more graciously observed than in home-loving Dorset. These good Dorset men were going direct to the Front, to the valley of the shadow of Death, to the very mouth of Hell. In a few days they would be thrown into a hideous riot of murder and death, and deafened with the roar of artillery and the crash of shells. They would find themselves in a scene of violence, or destruction and alarms such as Dante never dreamed of.

This was for a time at least – or possibly for ever – their last walk in the delectable county. Except from the train this was the last view they would have of that little corner of England they called their home. As they marched along they did not appear as individuals. The dim light made them indistinct. They were all dressed alike; they all marched alike; so that they seemed rather parts of a dull something that had hardly to do with men.

If one could have seen the pictures that flitted through their minds they would have been in strange contrast with the dreary scene. One pair of eyes saw a little cottage with a woman inside whose face was buried in her hands. Another saw a young girl waiting by a stile in the sun, a third a flock of sheep crossing a windy down, a fourth an empty blacksmith's forge with the fire still aglow on the hearth. They were walking among the dreams while of the dingy road they saw nothing ... I watched the draft until it was lost in the mist and until the horrible mocking music had almost died away.

Abbéville during the First World War, drawn by Dorset officer Capt. Brocklehurst.

Mr Dottery
By Theodore Francis Powys (1875-1953)

✳

Like his two celebrated author brothers, John and Llewelyn, Theodore Francis Powys loved Dorset passionately. Dorset was the county in which they had been happily raised and schooled by their rich clergyman father and well-connected mother in a family of eleven siblings; ultimately all three chose it for their last resting place. Theodore sets this cheeky and thought-provoking Christmas story in a fictitious and elemental Dorset village, a seemingly stagnant backwater where nothing appears to happen – and yet everything does. He reveals his delightful central character, the Reverend Mr Dottery, to be a world-weary philosopher and eccentric with a decided quirkiness of manner and a truly sardonic sense of humour.

A country church in snow on Christmas morning.

One can sometimes find, even in these merry days, an old gentleman living in the country, to whom a young and fair maiden is Anathema. Such a one was the Reverend Silas Dottery, a bachelor indeed, who has often affirmed in such a public place as the church pulpit at Tadnol, that had babies been born of trees — as Sir Thomas Browne once suggested — there would be no need of young women in the world, and what a crowning mercy that would be!

But, though Mr Dottery was a writer of history, he liked his dinner as well as his books, and preferred to read and dine alone, though sometimes a young man from the village would break in upon him and ask his advice about marriage and about young women. After giving wise and kind counsel, Mr Dottery would say — 'Ah, but it's a thousand pities that there are any of them — although to create a serviceable housekeeper like Mrs Taste and a cookmaid that is never seen, does in some ways recompense us for the mistaken kindness of the Almighty to man, when he made woman.'

'It's the cookmaid I've come about,' the young man usually answered.

'Marry her,' said Mr Dottery, 'and go.'

At breakfast, one gloomy morning, late in December, Mr Dottery — as he was wont to do, now and again, during this meal — looked at the letter bag that Mrs Taste had placed at the farther end of the table.

Mr Dottery, with the greatest care, poured out his third cup of tea, to which he added cream and sugar in abundance, and as he sipped the tea, he eyed with more than unwonted suspicion the bag, as though he supposed that a scorpion might be inside it. He expected indeed, the presence of a letter from his only sister, Mrs Clement — a married lady who had one child, a full-grown girl.

Mr Dottery didn't smoke — no real lover of old wine ever does — he sipped his next cup of tea, and after he had finished it, he unlocked the letter bag with a little sigh. Inside the bag there were two journals, four letters from old friends – one of them written in Latin – and another in a woman's hand that he knew only too well – his sister's.

'Oh!' Exclaimed Mr Dottery, with a groan, 'she must be having some trouble, and that's sure to be Barbara.' Mr Dottery opened the letter. 'Ever since that fool, Clement, had the indecency to die, Jane has written to me every week,' he said. 'At first it was only the measles or croup, but now it's always the young men. Was ever a scholar so tormented. But, what have we here?'

Mr Dottery was aghast. He read on.

'Why, she says,' he remarked in a horrified tone, waving the letter in the air, 'that if Sydney Napper were to find an opportunity to be with Barbara alone for ten minutes nothing could be done but marry them as soon as the banns could be read. He has only three pounds a week, one overcoat, a hearty appetite, and a moustache that can hardly be noticed. 'Sister Jane says that I must keep Barbara out of harm's way till after Christmas, when Sydney leaves the town.'

Mr Dottery rang the bell violently.

'The eggs, sir?' Said Mrs Taste, who entered immediately. 'I trust they were not hard boiled.'

'It's not the eggs, Mrs Taste,' replied Mr Dottery, 'It's something far worse than a mere misfortune of that nature, it's a young woman – it's Barbara.'

'She hasn't torn her clothes again?' Enquired Mrs Taste, with a matronly smile, 'for I remember when she stayed here two years ago, and was playing at run and hide with naughty Tommy in the farmer's barn–'

'Ah!' Said Mr Dottery, with a groan, 'I wish the barn had caught fire. It is not clothes now, Mrs Taste for Mrs Clement says that if Barbara should be left alone with Sydney Napper in any quiet place for only five minutes, the sooner the wedding bells were rung the better.'

'Oh, dear, dear!' Cried Mrs. Taste, 'if matters go as quick as that, I fear Miss Barbara will have nothing ready.'

'She comes here to-day,' moaned Mr Dottery, 'and I must lock her into her bedroom at night and never let her out of my sight for the daytime.' Mr Dottery looked so troubled and sad that Mrs Taste felt sorry for him.

'What must be done, sir?' she asked.

Mr Dottery looked up a little more happily. 'Send for the sexton,' he exclaimed, 'send for Sexton Truggin.'

Mrs. Taste turned pale. 'You don't mean that he should dig a grave for Miss Barbara?'

'No, Mrs. Taste,' replied Mr Dottery. 'I fear there is no chance of that; I only thought that, as Truggin is gardener here as well as sexton, she might be placed under his care. Be so kind as to call him.'

Mr Truggin wasn't far to seek; he was in the tool-shed, gazing at the mud upon his master's boots while he smoked contentedly.

'Truggin,' said Mr Dottery, 'you don't happen to have seen a large snake in the garden?'

'No,' replied Mr Truggin, 'taint the time of year for snakes or cuckoos.'

'I am glad of that,' said Mr Dottery, 'but are you able to watch a young woman?'

'I be able to watch and to do,' replied Mr Truggin.

'You mean, I suppose,' said Mr Dottery, 'that you are able to watch and also to protect my niece, Barbara, from harm, and so, Truggin, you must also see that she never goes out of the garden.'

'How about Sundays,' asked Mr Truggin, 'when we both be in church?'

'Barbara shall go too, Truggin,' said Mr Dottery, 'and as the Rectory pew is exactly under the pulpit, no harm can happen to her there.'

'One more word, Truggin,' said Mr Dottery, 'If you happen to hear a young gentleman caterwauling in the lane, be so good as to dig a grave for him.'

Mr Truggin slowly raised his finger, touched his forehead, and withdrew. Mr Truggin had only just time to escape safely unto the kitchen, when a pretty young creature, about eighteen years old, whose eyes were moist with crying, burst into Mr Dottery's study, and without saying 'by your leave' threw herself into his arms.

'But my dear,' said Mr Dottery, when Barbara drew back a little, 'you are wasting your pretty kisses.'

'Oh, Uncle Dottery,' cried Barbara, still holding her hands upon his shoulders and regarding him with all the wiles of a maiden who means to get her own way, 'Mother has been so unkind; she has not allowed me to see Sydney alone, and after Christmas he goes to America.'

'Forget him,' said Mr Dottery.

'But I love him,' moaned Barbara.

'Think of something else,' said Mr Dottery, 'for when I am disappointed of a plump pheasant for lunch, I often console myself with a bottle of good claret at dinner.'

'But Sydney isn't a plump pheasant, he is a young man,' replied Barbara.

'So your Mother has informed me,' observed Mr Dottery, drily.

'Mother is rude,' pouted Barbara. 'I can't tell you the behaviour she expects of us.'

'Ah, the way of sparrows,' sighed Mr Dottery.

Barbara stood beside the table, looking very pretty and sad. Her hands were folded innocently before her, and her eyes gazed tearfully at the floor. Mr Dottery observed her compassionately.

'A famous Spanish author once observed,' he said thoughtfully, 'that there is only one way for a young lady to take whose happiness depends upon her finding again her heart that she had lost, and that way is to discover some labour to do and to do it with all her might.'

'But what can I do?' Replied Barbara 'I hate making beds.'

Mr Dottery rang the bell, and Mrs. Taste softly opened the door.

'Miss Barbara,' observed Mr Dottery, 'would like, during her stay with us, to employ her time usefully.'

'There is plain sewing,' replied Mrs. Taste, respectfully, 'the young lady can hem the new sheets.'

'Oh,' sighed Barbara, 'I fear that kind of employment would only make me think the more of Sydney.'

Mr Dottery looked sadly at his boots and then at the study door.

'Christmas Day is next Friday,' remarked Mrs. Taste.

'How can Christmas Day help us?' Asked Mr Dottery, a little pettishly, 'for I am not editing the Holy Gospels, but the letters of Henry VIII.'

Barbara smiled.

'But the decorations,' said Mrs. Taste.

'You must remember, sir, that everyone complained about them last Christmas, because Truggin put holly in the pews instead of in the windows. Couldn't Miss Barbara trim the church and forget the young gentleman?'

Mr Dottery politely opened the study door.

'My dear Barbara,' he said happily, 'the Christmas decorations are just the thing for you. Green is good for the eyes, and yours look tearful. The church is almost in the Rectory garden – the side door is visible from my window – Truggin shall attend you. Do your best to make the Holy place look green and pretty.'

It was dark when Mr Truggin left the Rectory to go home to his own cottage, that was down a little narrow lane. A wider lane led to the Inn where a bright light burned. Unfortunately for Mr Truggin he had only empty pockets and so could not go to the light. He stood irresolutely, hoping that some chance might aid him to take the happy way. He was on the point of turning, in a very melancholy manner, towards his home, when a voice that was both gentle and low and seemed to come out of the lane hedge, enquired mournfully of Mr Truggin whether he had ever been in love.

'Have you ever been in love, Sexton?' Asked the voice, 'and have you ever been turned away from the door of your beloved by a hardhearted mother, who will not allow you to spend a few moments alone with the young lady?'

'No, never,' replied Mr Truggin, readily enough, 'for wold 'omen, who be mothers hereabout, don't say no to nothing – 'tis to be wished they did.'

Sexton Truggin now felt his right hand grasped tenderly in the darkness, and when he disengaged it, he discovered that his hand had not returned to him empty, but contained a crown piece. Mr Truggin walked towards the light...

Never had there been before such a lopping of green boughs in the Tadnol Rector's garden, as went on during the two days that were left before Christmas. The garden was full of evergreens and holly, and the little orchard that belonged to it was well stocked with mistletoe. Whenever Mr Dottery looked out of his window he beheld Mr Truggin and Barbara, climbing, sawing and chopping, and carrying what appeared to be half the green trees in the garden into the church.

Mr Dottery was pleased. Truggin proved an excellent guardian – no strange young man was ever seen to speak to Miss Barbara, and Mr

Dottery got on finely with his Latin letters. If he thought at all about the goings-on outside he thought pleasantly, for this year at least no-one would complain about the holly. Barbara had explained gaily that the only holly in the church would be placed around the pulpit.

Christmas morning came to gladden many a child's heart, and to bring to some others a gentle sadness, as they thought of former times when faith was stronger and simple minds were more eager to join in the glad tidings. But, though some bethought them of other days, all were ready enough to give gifts, to forget their cares, and to take a cheerful glass in honour of the grand birthday.

The Tadnol church bells rang merrily for the holy service that Mr Dottery held in the afternoon, and many went to hear the carols sung and the sermon preached.

Never, in the memory of the oldest inhabitant, had Tadnol church been so decked with greenery. The pulpit was so covered with red holly berries that Blacksmith Coot said it reminded him of the burning bush. The middle aisle was become a pretty shady walk, and the pews looked like so many green arbours upon each side of it. The rectory pew in particular, was so well hedged in by boughs of bay and laurel that no one who worshipped there could be seen at all.

When the last bell began to ring Uncle Dottery and his niece, Barbara, who smiled and looked happy, walked to church. Mr Dottery took the way to the vestry and Barbara, with a heightened colour, entered the rectory pew.

The service commenced and soon the joyful carols were being sung, and then it was noticed that the sound of two voices came from the rectory pew, singing most piously. Mr Dottery stepped into the pulpit and tried, by leaning forward a little, to see who was there, but the thick holly prevented him.

He began his sermon, that appeared to affect Miss Barbara in a curious manner, for from her hidden pew certain happy and abandoned sighs and other soft sounds came, denoting perhaps religious ecstasy.

Uncle Dottery turned in a hurry to the altar.

Christmas Poaching on the Lulworth Estate

✳

In the 'hungry twenties' (1820s) when inflation and high unemployment followed the end of the Napoleonic wars, poaching was an important supplement to the larder, especially over the Christmas period. Sir Robert Peel became Home Secretary in Lord Liverpool's Conservative government in 1822 and the same year rented Lulworth Castle and invited a group of friends to shoot on the estate in December. The Lulworth estate's gamekeeper heard a rumour that a band of poachers intended a midnight raid and he prepared to meet them with a force of twelve underkeepers and helpers. When the poachers were challenged they are said to have responded, 'We are five and thirty strong, and are for Death or Glory: but we will not use fire-arms unless your party fire first.' The battle was therefore fought with clubs and other implements and the gamekeeper's party was victorious, although he was injured. The poachers escaped that night, but several of them were later apprehended and four were transported to Australia — a decade before the transportation of the Tolpuddle Martyrs from Dorset to Australia.

Lulworth Castle, from Hutchins' *History.*

The White Donkey
By Benjamin Pond

✳

This classic ghost story is based on a first-hand encounter with a genuine Studland tradition. The story also features the delightful Studland pub, the Bankes Arms, which thankfully still survives, although the phantom donkey (as far as we know) is not currently visible!

It was back in December 1929 when in walking across the great Studland Heath near to midnight I suffered the most frightening experience of my whole life.

Back in those days I was a fisherman and if the tide was ebbing and there was but little wind I would sometimes leave my boat at Shell Bay at the mouth of Poole Harbour and walk the four miles across the heath to my shack at Goathorn.

No one lived within miles of the track I had to take nor were there even any roads; I had only a ten inch wide path trodden by wild cows when walking single file. These cows had escaped from distant crofts in years gone by.

This path, being of peat, would be almost black in colour and bordered by tall clumps of heather and brushwood. Being young and fit I thought nothing of doing this four mile walk, at least until a certain night, December 22nd.

That night I had moored my boat at Shell Bay at a late hour, somewhere about 11.30 and then begun my lonely walk. I had gone nearly one and a half miles when I saw a white object about 100 yards ahead, right in my path. I stopped; must be a sheet of newspaper perhaps, but I was a bit scared. How did it get there? There was no wind, yet it moved, but only slightly. By now I was really afraid.

I could not go on. It moved again. Then I decided to get into the heather and make a big half circle to avoid the object and so regain the path farther on. This I did. When I had gone about half-way I dared to look at the 'thing', and now I could see it broadside on, not end on as at first.

It was only a white donkey – but wait.

Now laughing at my fears, I regained the track and looked back, yes, there it stood, a white innocent donkey, or was it? Then suddenly it was gone, a complete disappearance. It was no more.

Again I was filled with doubts and fears; surely it could not have reached a clump of bushes sixty yards away and near to Bramble-Bush Bay. Nor was it just a sheet of paper as I had first imagined; perhaps that idea had come into my mind in thinking back to a night when someone had suspended long sheets of white paper in Poole Cemetery and some nearby residents were afraid to leave their homes for quite a time.

I hurried home. Surely if I returned that way in daylight I should find hoof marks on the soft peat and patches of sand. But next day when I came back to the spot there were *none*, not even one hoof indentation. No, never again would I tread this path again by night, I would take the shore route. I made this vow after certain facts came to light.

Determined to clear up the mystery – if it was a mystery – I went to all the crofters' holdings at the foot of Ballard Down; also to Corfe Castle, to see if anyone had allowed a white donkey to roam the heath; of more than forty donkeys in the area none was white.

A few months later I met Jim Coffin, fisherman, in the Banke's Arms, Studland, and to him I related the events of that awful night. He never interrupted until I finished my story, then he gave me a very odd look and said in a low voice, 'I too have seen that same donkey, 'tis there three days afore Christmas. I knows, came the heath way meself; was I afrighted? Not arf'.

He went on: 'You know old man Marsh, comes from Branksome to pick winkles and dig a bit o' bait; did sometimes sleep on Shell Bay side o' Harbour to be ready for early morn low tide, 'e too did see this donkey; so did some o' Riggs gang when they went to hide a load o' rum in Little-sea sedges'.

Old Coffin knew a lot more. He continued: 'Back along 160 years agone, a fellow was a riding a white donkey three nights afore Christmas near Bramble-Bush Bay when he was set on and murdered by a navy deserter who took his bag of money and a cask o' rum the poor feller had; the donkey ran away'.

Not so long ago I met old Peter Kaffie who was one of the real old salts and sailed round the world four times, now 82, and living back in Poole.

I said to him, 'Do you believe in spooks, ghosts?'

'Course I do, why not?' he replied.

'When and where did you see one?' I eagerly asked.

'Well, every Christmas Eve I do make it a 'abit to visit *every* pub on Poole Quay. Then feelin' sort o' 'appy like, I turns up 'igh Street to go 'ome and what do you think I sees up over Marine Stores? Why *two* ship's figure-heads instead o' one – she must 'ave a twin sister as only pays 'er a visit at Christmas. Funny fing, ain't it?'

The Bockhampton Band
Versus the Fordington Mummers
Christmas Eve 1828

From the Dorset County Chronicle, *24 January 1828*

Thomas Hardy's Uncle John was involved in this affray, which was a skirmish between two bands of Christmas entertainers. Clearly the Fordington Mummers thought that the Bockhampton Band was encroaching on their territory. John Hardy's associates, the Keates (who lived near the Hardys at Bockhampton), were attacked with a mummer's sword by the Fordington mummers, but it is unclear if the Bockhampton Band were mumming as well as playing and singing carols. Given Hardy's later interest in mumming and the statement in the 'Life' that he had seen a mummers' play in his youth, it would be fascinating to ascertain if there was a Bockhampton group of mummers involving the Hardy family as early as 1828.

John Lock, Joseph Lucas, James Burt, and George Burt, were indicted for creating a riot on the 24th Dec., and assaulting James Keates and Wm. Keates. As Counsel for the prosecution, Mr Gambier stated the case to the Jury, the circumstances of which were as follows:– It appears that for many years past, there has been a co-partnership or corporation composed of individuals, who assume to themselves the designation of the Fordington Mummers, and who conceive that they are entitled from their prescriptive right to a monopoly in their profession of affording

Above: Back view of Mill Street, Fordington in the nineteenth century. Photograph by Hermann Lea.

Right: Front view of Mill Street, Fordington in the nineteenth century. Photograph by Hermann Lea.

amusement to the good people of that parish and neighbourhood, during the convivial and merry-making time of Christmas. In the last year, however, a rival society has sprung up to pluck from them a portion of their laurels, in the neighbouring parish of Bockhampton, under the imposing title of the Bockhampton Band; and as the object of these latter was to afford a delicious titillation to the auricular nerves of the inhabitants of Bockhampton, Fordington, and the neighbourhood, by the performance of certain harmonious selections from the 'first composers', the profits of the honourable fraternity first mentioned were in a degree diminished. It was exceedingly natural that under this circumstance, a portion of hostility should exist; and as will be seen by

105

the subjoined evidence, this hostility ripened on Christmas-eve last, into what may be almost termed a 'battle royal'.

Joseph Keates sworn – is one of the Bockhampton band; knows Lucas and George Burt; they were with the mummers on Christmas-eve. John Lock and James Burt are Fordington mummers. About 10 o'clock, witness was passing between Swan Bridge and Gray's Bridge, with the rest of the band; they were all proceeding homewards very quietly; they were followed by the prisoners and about a dozen others who came up to them. Witness and a man named Hardy were carrying the drum, when Lucas came up, and said he would break the drum, and pulled off his coat wanting to fight. G. Burt also wanted to fight Hardy. Witness and Hardy attempted to get away, but were followed by the whole of the mummers' party and others, amounting then to about 100; who came up and surrounded the band. Witness received a severe blow on his body, one in the back of his head and a gash in his forehead with a sword, (this wound was very visible, and appeared of no inconsiderable extent). Witness was obliged to go to a surgeon. The conduct of all four of the prisoners was very noisy, outrageous, and abusive, and they swore very much.

William Keates, Charles Keates, and John Hardy, were called, who corroborated the evidence of the last witness, and also proved an assault on William Keates, and that the wound in James Keates's forehead was inflicted by James Burt.

[...] They were found guilty of the riot and assault, and were sentenced as follows – James Burt, six months' imprisonment and hard labour; George Burt, John Lock, and Joseph Lucas, three months' imprisonment and hard labour.

Robin Redbreast: The Bird of the Christmas Card

By Denys Watkins-Pritchford

The author's reference to the robin as being a bird of 'ill omen' is borne out in folklore, in which it is a harbinger of death. A Dorset example of this is the account of a robin tapping on the window of Lawrence of Arabia's cottage shortly before his death. The robin may originally have been a sacrificial bird like the wren, as indicated in the ancient ballad of 'The Death and Burial of Cock Robin' found in many European languages. The robin's red breast gave rise to several legends, such as the story that he received it through being pricked by the crown of thorns while trying to remove it from Christ's head, or that he burnt his breast in bringing the gift of fire to man. These stories of the robin being helpful to man at first do not seem to equate with him being a bird of ill-omen, but lore does suggest his help of mankind, despite being involved as a presager of disaster. An interesting example comes in the folk tale and pantomime Babes in the Wood *where the robins, too late to save the lives of the babes , preserve the bodies from the wild beasts to protect their souls – a very ancient concept indeed which is the basis of Sophocles' play* Antigone.*

What a strange thing it is to read that our familiar and much loved robin was once regarded as a bird of ill omen.

Yet this was so in the south of England during the last century, and in other parts of the country also. This may have been due to the old superstition which associated the robin with the Crucifixion. The red

A Victorian
Christmas card.

on the robin's breast was due to the fact that the little bird was supposed to have visited Our Lord upon the Cross and tried to staunch the wounds.

Despite this belief, robins singing near a house were considered unlucky yet no man dare harm them, indeed, he who slew a robin was sure to have bad luck. Even birdnesting village boys think twice before harming a robin or touching its eggs. In this more enlightened age we think no more of these old wives tales, the robin is universally beloved, and his bright orange waistcoat (which is not of course red at all) makes a gay spot of colour, as cheerful as a holly berry in the winter landscape.

Over the ages robins have frequented the dwellings of man and have won his love by their fearlessness and friendliness. When Christmas Cards became popular in the latter part of the last century, the redbreast came into his own. We always associate robins with winter and Christmastime, it is always depicted in snow scenes, though sometimes the bird is unrecognisable save for its bright vermilion breast which the hack-work artist insists on giving it.

There is another trait in its character which makes us love it, its trickling little song which is about the only bird song we can hope to hear in the bleak and sunless days. Actually robins have a longer song period than any other British bird. They sing from October to July and in those months they cease to sing only for about a fortnight or three weeks. By mid autumn they are again in full song and it is then perhaps we notice the song the most.

When in late October or early November we have a day of sun, that golden sun which filters through to the woodland floor and seems to light the dead membrances of each leaf with hidden fire then the robin comes into his own. Many may be heard singing, each in its own territory, for it is a jealous bird and will tolerate no other on its own ground. How strangely poignant that song is, full of wistful sadness which is so in accord with autumn and the year's end.

There is a belief that robins' nests are easy to find because they build in odd corners about the garden, preferring to nest in a dark nook, in some cavity in a wall, upturned flower pot, or even, as sometimes happens, on the head of a rake, or in the pocket of an old jacket. Our old gardener whose name was Gunn kept a very ancient discarded jacket hanging behind a door in the potting shed and a robin built a nest in the pocket. We never discovered this until the young were ready to leave the nest and by accident knocked against the jacket. The young burst forth in all directions.

In August robins are busy fighting over their territories, establishing their claims for the coming season, and the males mate in late December and not in spring, as is generally supposed.

I had an instance of the tender devotion of a cock robin to its mate last spring. I had noticed a puffed–up robin haunting the shrubbery by my garden pool, it hardly moved out of my way and if I came too close gave but a feeble

109

flutter. Its mate was in attendance and whenever came near he set up a great commotion and seemed very anxious. From time to time he perched near his sick wife singing to her and was never far away.

Soon she was too feeble to feed and then I saw that he was feeding her with great tenderness, searching for special titbits which he gave to her very gently. It was most touching to see his concern. Perhaps the fact that it was high spring which made the little scene all the more poignant for the trees were bursting into leaf and all the green world of garden and wood were awakening.

For three days he fed her but all the time she grew weaker until at last, one day, I found her lying dead and her mate had gone.

Those robins which build away from houses are very clever at concealing their nests, indeed a robin's nest is very difficult to find, and even if you watch the parent birds, they are wary of giving away their secret.

They share this wariness with their close relation the nightingale, which bird builds in very similar situations, on the ground in thick cover.

Not many people know the alarm note of the robin when you are close to its young. It is one of the most sorrowful sounds I know, it wrings the heart.

Another curious trait is its passion for bathing and the time chosen is very odd, often at the very edge of the dark.

The day may have been bitterly cold and frosty, a clammy fog cloaks the garden, the winter's night has almost come, but often I see, in the fast gathering shadows, a robin bathing vigorously in the garden pool, not half-heartedly dabbling its toes in the icy water, but throwing the freezing moisture over itself and getting thoroughly wet. In this wet state they retire to roost, almost always singly.

I know of no other bird which is about so late in winter or who bathes so late.

The Sherborne Missal

✳

*One of the most surprising illustrations of a Christmas robin comes in a priceless
and very weighty medieval book now in the collection of the British Library. This
is the Sherborne Missal, which was written between the years 1399 and 1407
in the scriptorium of the Benedictine Abbey of St Mary's, Sherborne as their
mass-book. The text is in Latin and the scribe, John Whas, was a member of the
Benedictine community at Sherborne; the missal also contains music for the mass.
Each one of its 690 vellum pages (38cm by 54.3cm) is enhanced with pictorial*

John Siferwas's illustration of
a robin in the margin of the
Sherborne Missal.

decoration — there are marginal decorations, initial letters and paintings in the form of miniatures portraying saints, angels, kings, noblemen, bishops, abbots and monks. More unusually for the period, particularly regarding the nature of the servicebook, there are in addition forty-eight images of British birds, each labelled with their Middle English name, adorning the Ordinary and Canon of the Mass. Responsible for the bird paintings was the missal's principal artist, the Dominican friar John Siferwas, who worked with four assistants. The book's production was sponsored by Abbot Robert Bruning (or Bruyning) and Richard Mitford, Bishop of Sherborne.

Sherborne Cross, Market Place, *c.* 1900. Photograph by Hermann Lea.

Smugglers' Booty in Langton Church

By William Masters Hardy

✷

The long dark nights of midwinter around new moon were excellent for the smuggling activities of the Dorset coast which were so vital to the local economy before the growth of free trade in the mid-nineteenth century removed the impetus for import smuggling of spirits, tea and tobacco.

In December 1819 a Revenue cutter at Weymouth captured three smuggling ships on the same day; the Revenue men impounded 298 casks of spirits and three casks of tea. The following day the Revenue cutter capsized in a heavy gale and four of the five men on board were saved by a flotilla of small boats, 'some manned by smugglers'!

Langton, on the Isle of Purbeck, was home to a famous gang of smugglers and one of the most famous stories about them concerns Christmas 1830, not many years before free trade put an end to the traditional forms of smuggling.

At one time there were a number of people in Langton and the neighbourhood well known to be great smugglers. About the year 1830 an exciting incident happened at this church.

Most of the smugglers' hiding places had become well known to the Coastguards. Another place had to be found somewhere. So a few Langtonian smugglers had a consultation, and one of the head ones thought he knew a first-rate place, which was over the ceiling of the church in the apex of the roof. The place was reached by going up inside the tower. This new place was used for smuggling for a long time before it was discovered.

One dark night in December they were expecting a cargo of tubs in at Dancing Ledge. The ganger and his men were all on the Ledge watching for their craft. They had not to wait long before she came. They got the tubs ashore all right, and away went the boat to sea again in the darkness. The smugglers were glad to see their tubs landed safe without the Coastguards seeing them. They were men of different callings – quarriers, masons, labourers, shepherds, &c.

The ganger said to them, 'Now, my lads, I can see very clearly that we shall not be able to get this big freight of tubs stored in the church tonight, seeing that all our men have not turned up. We shall have to stow them in some spot near the church. I do not know what to do.'

Then a quarrier suggested putting the kegs in an old quarry near Spyway. Some did not agree with this place, because it was wet and dirty. At last the ganger said to a farm labourer 'Come, Tom, don't you know a place handy? We have taken your advice before and it has been all right.' 'Yes,' said Tom, 'I know a good spot down at Spyway barn. Pack them over with some straw.' 'Oh!' they said, 'the Coastguard will be sure to find them there.' 'No,' said Tom, 'I will take good care of that. I will open the bullhouse door and let the bull out night and day all the time they are

Coastguard's house on
Pevril Point.

The Hawkhurst smuggling gang from Kent breaking open the Customs House at Poole.

there. As you all know, our bull is a terror to the neighbourhood, and no one will ever go near him – not even the brave Coastguard with their brace of pistols, cutlasses, muskets, and fixed bayonets.' 'Very well,' said the ganger, 'we will take your advice, Tom.' Then, before they began to work, they sat down and drank some of the hot stuff to spur them up over the cliff. Afterwards they went to work like dragons, first having placed two watchmen, one on the east, and the other on the west. They got their tubs all up over the cliff and down to the barton at Spyway, where they left them in the custody of 'John Bull'. After this the men sat down and finished the remainder of the spirits left in the little keg that they had opened on Dancing Ledge. Then they all went home to bed and did not get up before twelve o' clock next day.

The next evening they were all summoned to the private room of the King's Arms to devise plans to finish the job. The ganger said 'We must have a different plan from last time, for although it was very dark we only just escaped capture. We ought not to have unloaded the waggon in front of the Church. This time we must get to the tower another way.' One said that they might bring the waggon down Durnford Road and get through the garden at the back of the house and through a small door west of the tower. The ganger answered 'That is a very good plan; but I see two great lions in the way. First, there is old John the gardener. He will tell the Squire everything and a little more.' 'Leave him to me,' said the landlord, who was a bit of a smuggler himself, 'I will get him to leave the garden gate unlocked. I know the way to square old John.' 'Well,' said the ganger, 'That is one lion dead. What about the other? There is a great dog whose kennel is close to the door.' At this the shepherd spoke up and said 'I can kill that lion, for I had a sheep die the other day, so I can give that dog something to do for an hour.' Then said the ganger 'I think this plan will do very well. We must all meet at the barton to-morrow night.' So they all met at Spyway, loaded up the waggon, putting a little straw on the top, and at last the tubs were safely stowed away in the Church. Nothing happened until three weeks after, when it was thought that one of the gang got short of cash and went over to Poole and gave information, for which he received £50. The next day Mr Lander, the chief Customs House officer, came to Swanage and called at Mr Nat Chinchen's, at the Old Bank. Mr Chinchen asked him to stay to lunch, but he said that he could not stop, as he had information that there was a large quantity of tubs packed away in Langton Church, and he must go and take charge of them at once. This he did, and took them all away next day. I do not think that Langton Church was ever used for smuggling after that.

Dancing Ledge, used by the Langton smugglers. Photograph by Geoff Doel.

The Symondsbury Mummers' Play

From John Udal's Dorsetshire Folk-lore *(1922).*

Both William Barnes and Thomas Hardy had seen mummers' plays in their youth and they both considered them to be relics of the medieval crusading period, dramatising the conflict with the Turks in the Holy Land. Barnes describes them in 1863 as:

> a set of youths who go about at Christmas, decked with painted paper and tinsel, and act in the houses of those who like to receive them a little drama, mostly, though not always, representing a fight between St George and a Mohammedan leader, and commemorative, therefore of the Holy Wars. One of the characters, with a hump-back and bawble, represents 'Old Father Christmas'.

The classic, and often quoted, account of a Dorset mummers' play is that of Hardy in The Return of the Native, *where his daring heroine, Eustacia Vye, enters a male preserve by taking the part of the Turkish Knight. One of the combatants, Jim Starks, is clearly based on Hardy's cousin Jim Sparks at Puddletown, which gives the clue to the likely context of Hardy seeing the play. Hardy quoted part of the text in the novel and in later life he gathered together other fragments and rewrote what he could not remember or acquire from others. In the novel, Hardy describes the costumes and the hard work of 'sisters and sweethearts' in this area; and he distinguished the Doctor with 'his darker habiliments, peculiar hat, and the bottle of physic' and Father Christmas (played by an older man):*

The village of Symondsbury, from Hutchins' *History*.

Meanwhile Jim Starks as the Valiant Soldier had come forward, and, with a glare upon the Turk replied –

If, then, thou art that Turkish Knight,
Draw out thy sword, and let us fight!

And fight they did; the issue of the combat being that the Valiant Soldier was slain by a preternaturally inadequate thrust from Eustacia, Jim, in his ardour for genuine histrionic art, coming down like a log upon the stone floor with force enough to dislocate his shoulder. Then, after more words from the Turkish Knight, rather too faintly delivered, and statements that he'd fight Saint George and all his crew, Saint George himself magnificently entered with the well-known flourish –

Here come I Saint George, the valiant man,
With naked sword and spear in hand,

[After killing the Turk] The play proceeded between Saint George, the Saracen, the Doctor and Father Christmas.

The Dorset folklorist John Udal collected a rather different play from Symondsbury, which was regularly performed until the First World War and revived in 1953 (when it was filmed) and has again been regularly performed since. In this version, St George and St Patrick fight four combatants with symbolic but non-crusading names, after which Dr Martin Denis mixes a special potion to bring them back from the dead – a midwinter resurrection typical of most mummers' plays. There are a further three parts to the play which we have not quoted, including a hobby horse perhaps similar to that mentioned by Hardy's father in an earlier quote.

Arthur Hopkins' illustration of the mummers' rehearsal for *The Return of the Native*.

Personae
Old Father Christmas
Room
Anthony, the Egyptian King
St George
St Patrick
Captain Bluster
Gracious King
General Valentine
Colonel Spring
Doctor

Scene: The servants' hall or kitchen of the mansion or farmhouse in which the performance is to take place. The actors are grouped together at the back of the stage, so to speak, and each comes forward as he is required to speak or to fight; and at the conclusion falls back upon the rest, leaving the stage clear for other disputants or combatants. This is the 'enter' and 'exit' of the mummers.

Enter Old Father Christmas:
Here comes I, Father Christmas, welcome or welcome not,
I hope Old Father Christmas will never be forgot.
Although it is Old Father Christmas he has but a short time to stay;
I am come to show you pleasure and pass the time away.
I have been far, I have been near,
And now I am come to drink a pot of your Christmas beer;
And if its a pot of your best,
I hope in heaven your soul will rest.
If it is a pot of your small
We cannot show you no Christmas at all.
Walk in, Room, again I say,
And pray, good people, clear the way.
Walk in, Room.

Enter Room:
God bless you all, ladies and gentlemen,

It's Christmas time, and I am come again.
My name is Room, one sincere and true;
A merry Christmas I wish to you.
King of Egypt is for to display,
A noble champion without delay.
St Patrick too, a charming Irish youth,
He can fight or dance, or love a girl with truth.
A noble Doctor I do declare, and his surprising tricks bring up the rear.
And let the Egyptian King straightway appear.

Enter Egyptian King:
Here comes I, Anthony, the Egyptian King,
With whose mighty acts all round the globe doth ring;
No other champion but me excels,
Except St George, my only son-in-law;
Indeed that wondrous knight whom I so dearly love,
Whose mortal deeds the world dost well approve,
That hero whom no dragon could affright,
A whole troop of soldiers couldn't stand in sight.
Walk in, St. George, his warlike ardour to display,
Walk in St. George and show us British play!

Enter St George:
Here am I, St George, an Englishman so stout,
With these mighty warriors I long to have a bout;
No one could ever picture me the many I have slain,
I long to fight, it's my delight, the battle o'er again.
Come, then, you boasting champions,
And hear that in war I doth take pleasure,
I will fight you all, both great and small,
And slay you at my leisure.
Come haste away, make no delay,
For I'll give you some lusty thumps,
And like a true-born Englishman
I'll fight you on my stumps.
And now the world I do defy
To injure me before I die.

So now prepare for war, for that is my delight.

Enter St Patrick, who shakes hands with St George.

St Patrick:
My worthy friend, how dost thou fare, St George?
Answer my worthy knight.

St George:
I am glad to find thee here;
In many a fight that I have been in, travelled far and near,
To find my worthy friend St Patrick, that man I love so dear.
Four bold warriors have promised me
To meet me here this night to fight.
The challenge I did accept, but they could not me affright.

St Patrick:
I will always stand by that man who did me first enlarge,
I thank thee now in gratitude, my worthy friend, St Garge;
Thou did'st first deliver me out of this wretched den,
And now I have my liberty I thank thee once again.

Enter Captain Bluster:
I'll give St George a thrashing, I'll make him sick and sore,
And if I further am disposed I'll thrash a dozen more.

St Patrick:
Large words, my worthy friend,
St George is here.
And likewise St Patrick too,
And he doth scorn such men as you;
I am the match for thee.
Therefore prepare yourself to fight with me,
Or else I'll slay thee instantly.

Captain Bluster:
Come on, my boy! I'll die before
I yield to thee, or twenty more.

They fight, and St Patrick kills Captain Bluster.

St Patrick:
Now one of St George's foes is killed by me,
Who fought the battle o'er;
And now for the sake of good St George,
I'll freely fight a hundred more.

St George:
No, no, my worthy friend, St George is here,
I'll fight the other three;
And after that with Christmas beer
So merry we will be.

Enter Gracious King:
No beer or brandy, Sir, I want my courage for to rise,
I only want to meet St George or take him by surprise;
But I am afraid he never will fight me;
I wish I could that villain see.

St George:
Tremble, thou tyrant, for all thy sin that's past,
Tremble to think that this night will be thy last.
Thy conquering arms shall quickly by thee lay alone,
And send thee passing to eternal doom.
St George will make thy armour ring;
St George will soon despatch the Gracious King.

Gracious King:
I'll die before I yield to thee or twenty more.

They fight. St George kills the Gracious King. Enter General Valentine.

St George:
He was no match for me, he quickly fell.

General Valentine:
But I am thy match, and that my sword shall tell.
Prepare thyself to die, and bid thy friends farewell.
I long to fight such a brave man as thee,

For it's a pleasure to fight so manfully.
Thou art no coward, but a man so brave,
Battle so severe I long to have.
So cruel, for thy foes are always killed!
Oh! What a sight of blood St George has spilled!
I'll fight St George, the hero, here,
Before I sleep this night.
Come on, my boy, I'll die before
I yield to thee or twenty more.
St George, thou and I'll the battle try,
If thou dost conquer I will die.

They fight. St George kills the General.

St George:
Where now is Colonel Spring? He doth so long delay,
That hero of renown, I long to show him play.

Enter Colonel Spring:
Holloa! behold me, here am I!
I'll have thee now prepare,
And by this arm thou'lt surely die,
I'll have thee this night beware.
So see what bloody works thou'st made,
Thou art a butcher, sir, by trade.
I'll kill thee as thou didst my brother,
For one good turn deserves another.

St George:
Come, give me leave, I'll thee battle,
And quickly make thy bones to rattle.

Colonel Spring:
Come on, my boy, I'll die before
I'll yield to thee or twenty more.
St George, thee and I
Will the battle try.

They fight. St George kills the Colonel.

St Patrick:
Stay thy hand, St. George, and slay no more; for I feel for the wives and families of those men that you have slain.

St George:
So am I sorry. I'll freely give any sum of money to a doctor to restore them again. I have heard talk of a mill to grind old men young, but I have never heard of a doctor to bring dead men to life again.

St Patrick:
There's an Irish doctor, a townsman of mine, who lived next door to St Patrick; he can perform wonders. Shall I call him, St. George?

St George:
With all my heart.

St Patrick:
Please to walk in Mr Martin Dennis. It's an ill wind that blows no good work for the doctor.

Enter Doctor.

St George:
If you will set these men on their pins, I'll give thee a hundred pound, and here is the money.

Doctor:
So I will, my worthy knight, and then I shall not want for whiskey for one twelvemonth to come. I am sure the first man I saw beheaded I put his head on the wrong way. I put his mouth where his poll ought to be, and he's exhibited as a wonder of nature.

St George:
Very good answer, Mr Doctor. Tell me the rest of your miracles, and raise those warriors.

Doctor:
I can cure love-sick maidens, jealous husbands, squalling wives, brandy-drinking dames, with one touch of my purple liquid or one sly dose of my Jerusalem balsam; and that will make an old crippled dame dance the hornpipe, or an old woman of seventy years of age conceive and bear a twin.

And now to convince you all of my exertions, rise Captain Bluster, Gracious King, General Valentine, and Colonel Spring! Rise, and go to your father!

On the application of the medicine they all rise and retire.

The Hardy Players performing the *Play of St George* in the early twentieth century.

Christmas Carollers
By William Masters Hardy

About six weeks before Christmas, the church singers used to meet and practise hymns, carols &c, in a cottage near 'The Monument'. One of the carols then sung was composed by the Rev. T.O. Bartlett, the Rector, and another by the late Mr Thos. Manwell. The singing was always accompanies by a small band consisting of the following instrumentalists: Mr James Manwell (first fiddle), Mr Jos. Curtis and Mr Stephen Masters (first clarionets), Mr Jos Mowlem (second clarinet), Mr W.M. Hardy (also clarionet), Mr Matthew Gillingham (violoncello), and Mr Daniell Summers (bass trombone). Mr Geo. Stickland sang bass, and other members of the choir were representatives of the families of Coleman, Chinchen, Thomes, Melmoth, Manwell &c. There were 17 in all. After the usual amount of practice the band and singers turned out in full strength on Christmas Eve, and having, as a rule, marched to the Globe, at Herston, they commenced their harmonious entertainment by the generous landlord, Mr Geo. Fooks. The merry party then proceeded to Newton Cottage, halted to serenade the residents with a few carols, and then went on to Court Farm to give Farmer John Smith a taste of their quality. Thence they returned to Mr Samuel Marsh's on Church Hill; then went to the Rev. H. Jackson at the Rectory, where the butler, Mr Sweet, rewarded the thirsty performers with the best of the cellar's contents. Retracing their steps they paid Magnolia House, then occupied by the late Dr. Delamotte. Continuing their musical march, the next halt was made at the Red Lion, where the landlord Mr Wm

Vye dispensed the customary refreshments. Another halt was made lower down opposite the Old Bank, occupied by the late Mr W.G. White and just below, on the opposite side of the road, Mr T. Randell, stone merchant, was regaled with a selection of carols. The Anchor Inn was next visited, and there the landlord Mr Wm. Hatchard, did the honours as a generous host. The White Swan came in for attention next, the landlord being Mr E. Vatcher. Still further down, Mr James Craft, the Customs House officer and Captains T. Masters and James Edmonds and Mr John Mowlem, of Victoria Terrace, were serenaded. The Victoria Hotel, kept then by Mr Richard Rowe; Captain McKenzie of Osborne House; the Rev. J.M. Colson, of Belvedere; and Mrs Coventry, of The Grove, were next visited in turn, until finally the energetic and untiring songsters and musicians ended their arduous march and exertions at the now non-existent Brewery, where refreshments were liberally offered and as liberally indulged in. By this time, five o'clock in the morning, the waits were weary, and then retired to their several homes for a much needed rest until the bells, ringing for the afternoon's service, called them to play and sing the hymns and carols from the gallery situated at the west end of the old church. Their musical endeavours were accompanied by the organist, on the old organ, and at this service were to be seen nearly all the inhabitants able to attend, not only the regular church-goers, but Congregationalists, Wesleyans, and others who were not members of any recognised church, this being the way they showed their appreciation of the festive season.

On Boxing Days the waits used to meet together and go round and wait upon the principal tradesmen and farmers. Commencing at Whitecliff Farm in the morning, they went to Godlingston Farm, and thence to Herston, again passing in succession the various houses previously mentioned, until they finally wound up at the Brewery, where

their thirst was quenched, and the money which had been collected on the way was distributed among the singers and players.

Mr Smith's Public Ball at the Antelope

From 'Before You Were Born' in the South Times, *1 December 1939*

This account lists some of the more popular social dances taught to young persons in the mid-nineteenth century by professional Dancing Masters. However, it is not surprising that Mr Smith has neither introduced his young ladies and gentlemen to the exciting polka which hailed from Paris via Bohemia and was all the rage in the 1840s, nor the waltz – both were for a considerable time disapproved of in respectable circles. One of the 'gems of the evening' (and most appreciated by the 'large and respectable assembly') was the sailor's hornpipe, which remained popular throughout the nineteenth century; this was England's original contribution to the dance form and carried overtones of nationalism.

It afforded an opportunity to a large and respectable assembly of the inhabitants of this town and its vicinity, of witnessing the attainment of [Mr Smith's] pupils, in the stately quadrille, the brilliant *galope*, and the eccentric *mjourka*; the chaste and finished style of their dancing, their multifarious evolutions though the mazy dance together with the adjuncts of a full room and an excellent band presented an ensemble truly delightful. A *galope* of eight ladies, and a *mjourka* and hornpipe by a young gentleman were the gems of the evening. After the pupils had concluded, the dancing became general and continued till a very late hour, when the company separated highly pleased with the gratification thus afforded them and the attentions of Mr Smith as MC.

The Antelope
Hotel, *c.* 1840.

A children's
dance.

Grammer's Shoes

By William Barnes

A poignant and affectionate family Christmas poem from
William Barnes' dialect collection.

I do seem to zee Grammer as she did use
Vor to show us, at Chris'mas, her wedden shoes,
An' her flat spreaden bonnet so big an' roun
As a girt pewter dish a-turn'd upside down;
When we all did draw near
In a cluster to hear
O' the merry wold soul how she did use
To walk an' to dance wi' her high-hell shoes.

She'd a gown wi' girt flowers lik' hollyhocks,
An' zome stockens o' gramfer's a-knit wi' clocks,
An' a token she kept under lock an' key, –
A small lock ov his heair off avore't wer grey.

An' her eyes wer red,
An' she shook her head,
When we'd all a-look'd at it, an' she did use
To lock it away wi' her wedden shoes.

She could tell us such teales, about heavy snows,
An' o' rains an' o' floods when the waters rose
All up into the housen, an' carr'd awoy
All the bridge wi' a man an' his little bwoy;
An' o' vog an' vrost,
An' o' vo'k a-lost,

An' o' pearties at Chris'mas, when she did use
Vor to walk hwome wi' gramfer in high-heel shoes.

Ev'ry Chris'mas she lik'd vor the bells to ring,
An' to have in the zingers to hear em zing
The wold carols she heard many years a-gone,
While she warm'd em zome cider avore the bron';
An' she'd look an' smile
At our dancen, while
She did tell how her friends now a-gone did use
To reely wi' her in their high-heel shoes.

Ah! An' how she did like vor to deck wi' red
Holly-berries the window an' wold clock's head,
An' the clavy wi' boughs o' some bright green leaves,
An' to meake twoast an' eale upon Chris'mas eves;
But she's now, drough greace,

In a better pleace,

Though we'll never vorget her, poor soul, nor lose

Gramfer's token ov heair, nor her wedden shoes.

A statue of William Barnes in
Dorchester (photograph by
Geoff Doel).

The Purbeck Apparition
By Revd John Hutchins

In December 1678, the owner of Creech Grange, near Wareham, and his brother rode to London to inform the Council that an army several thousand strong had landed on the Dorset coast and had been sighted by many people in the Wareham area. The brothers were seemingly mistaken, but the episode made such a strong impression locally and so many people claimed to have seen the army that a supernatural basis for the tale has been posited. The army was seen with clashing weapons marching along the crest of the Purbeck Hills above Creech Grange, which originally belonged to the Cistercian monks of Bindon Abbey and Christmas religious and social preparations were forgotten and the militia gathered to defeat the invading forces.

The story is told in Revd John Hutchins's The History and Antiquities of the County of Dorset *(1773). John Hutchins (1698-1773) was vicar of Wareham so was local to these events and gathered traditions to them. His county history was his life's work and was dedicated posthumously to his wife Anne, who risked her life ten years earlier to save her husband's manuscripts from a fire. The history has been enormously influential and was a major source used by Thomas Hardy; the historical narratives are enlivened by the inclusion of stories such as the one given below. Two further editions were produced after Hutchins' death, the normally used one today being William Shipp's substantially augmented edition of 1861-70.*

On top of the hill, south of and opposite to Mr Bond's house, (Creech Grange) a very remarkable phenomenon was pretended to have appeared in 1678. One evening in Dorchester was imagined to be seen a vast number of armed men, several thousands, marching from Flower's Barrow over Grange

Hill, and a great noise and clashing of arms was supposed to have been heard. Nothing appeared on the south side of the hill. They were pretended to have been seen by Captain John Lawrence, then owner of the Grange, who lived there, and his brother, and 100 more, particularly by four clay-cutters, just going to leave off work and by all the people in the cottages and hamlets thereabouts, who left their supper and houses, and came to Wareham, and alarmed the town, on which the boats were all drawn to the north side of the river, and the bridge barricaded. Three hundred of the militia were marched to Wareham. Captain Lawrence and his brother went post to London, and deposed the particulars on oath before the Council, and, had not he and his family been of known affection to the government, he would have been severely punished, the nation being in a ferment about Oates's plot. This account I had from one Thomas Bolt, a native of Wareham, who then lived there, and perfectly remembered the particulars; he died in 1758, aged 59.

I have in my possession an original letter written by Mr Thomas Dolman, I suppose then Clerk of the Council, dated Dec. 14, 1678, directed to George Fulford and Robert Coker, esqrs. officers of the militia, wherein he tells them that Mr Secretary Coventry had communicated their letter of the 10th instant, touching the number of armed men pretended to be seen in Purbeck, to the Lords of the Council, who commanded him to let them know that they tok in good part their care in putting themselves in a posture of defence, and that the contrivers and spreaders of this false news were ordered to be sent for, to be dealt with according to their deserts.

[...] In a collection of State Tracts, 1706 ... is a pamphlet, published in 1679, containing arguments against a standing army. It has a few hints of this affair, which the author sometimes treats with contempt, calling it the Purbeck apparition, yet makes it an argument for a militia, and says above 40,000 armed volunteers assembled in two or three days' time to have met the French had they been there, but that the court disliked it, and questioned the sheriff about it. This looks as if the 'posse comitatus' was then raised. In 1756 this trifling story was revived, and made an argument for the necessity and usefulness of a militia.

This phenomenon seems to have been owing to the thick fogs and mists that often hang on the hills in Purbeck, and form grotesque appearances of large craggy rocks and ruins of buildings. At this time the evening sun might glance on these, which, assisted and improved by a strong imagination, caused the spectators to fancy what never existed.

Creech Grange, from Hutchins' *History*.

East view of Bindon Abbey, from Hutchins' *History*.

The Tranter's Christmas Party
From Under the Greenwood Tree *by Thomas Hardy*

Under the Greenwood Tree (1872) was Thomas Hardy's second published novel and led to his talents being spotted by Leslie Stephen, who serialised later work in the prestigious Cornhill Magazine. *Stephen was attracted by Hardy's ability to present idiosyncratic and picturesque rural life to an urban audience with insight, compassion and humour; the challenge to sexual and social mores and the dark tragic vein had not yet entered Hardy's published writings.*

Under the Greenwood Tree, like many of Hardy's works, gives prominence to the passing of the seasons, and is particularly delightful in its exposition of Christmas. There is a wonderful description of the quire progressing round the parish of Mellstock on Christmas Eve and playing to the householders, followed by the same quire, in a rather tired state, playing below their best during the Christmas Day services, which ultimately leads to their displacement. In the evening the tranter gives a party for the Quire and neighbours and it is this extract we have selected. The Mellstock Quire is of course based on the Stinsford Quire run by the Hardy family which was disbanded around 1843 from its church obligations. But the quire musicians continued with their secular playing at parties. The Hardy family manuscript music books reflect this and in his introduction to the novel Hardy says 'It was customary to inscribe a few jigs, reels, hornpipes, and ballads in the same book, by beginning it at the other end, the insertions being continued from front and back till sacred and secular met together in the middle, often with bizarre effect'.

In his boyhood Hardy often played with his father's dance band and was thus intimately acquainted with the dances and the mode of playing for them. Hardy uses the dance 'Follow My Lover' symbolically to show, very humorously, the rival courtship of Dick and Farmer Shiner for Fancy Day, the figures of the dance being emblematic of changing

patterns of rivalry in love. Mr Shiner, having secured Fancy, won't cast off 'for any man'
and so prolongs his pleasure with Fancy. Although Dick has the pleasure of dancing at
length with Fancy in the final dance, this is undercut by Shiner seeing her home, since
Dick, as host, has to stay put!

The interesting Dorset tradition in some areas of not allowing dancing on Christmas
Day is shown in this extract, with Old William not allowing the dancing to start until
midnight. At the end of the dance, Mrs Penny recounts a Dorset husband divination
custom. Although her experience is from Old Midsummer's Eve, the custom was part of
solstitial divination practices, which were also appropriate to New Year.

The guests had all assembled, and the tranter's party had reached that
degree of development which accords with ten o'clock p.m. In rural
assemblies. At that hour the sound of a fiddle in process of tuning was
heard from the inner pantry.

'That's Dick,' said the tranter. 'That lad's crazy for a jig.'

'Dick!' Now I cannot – really, I cannot have any dancing at all till
Christmas Day is out,' said old William emphatically. 'When the clock
ha' done striking twelve, dance as much as ye like.'

'Well, I must say there's reason in that, William,' said Mrs Penny. 'If you
do have a party on Christmas night, 'tis only fair and honourable to the
Church to have it a sit-still party. Jigging parties be all very well, and this,
that, and therefore; but a jogging party looks suspicious now. O yes; stop
till the clock strikes, young folk – so say I.'

It happened that some warm mead accidentally got into Mr Spinks's
head about this time. 'Dancing,' he said, 'is a most strengthening,
livening, and courting movement, 'specially with a little beverage added!
And dancing is good. But why disturb what is ordained, Richard and
Reuben, and the company zhinerally? Why, I ask, as far as that do go?'

'Then nothing till after twelve,' said William.

Though Reuben and his wife ruled on social points, religious questions were mostly disposed of by the old man, whose firmness on this head quite counterbalanced a certain weakness in his handling of domestic matters. The hopes of the younger members of the household were therefore relegated to a distance of one hour and three quarters – a result that took visible shape in them by a remote and listless look about the eyes – the singing of songs being permitted in the interim.

At five minutes to twelve the soft tuning was again heard in the back quarters; and when at length the clock had whizzed forth the last stroke, Dick appeared ready primed, and the instruments were boldly handled; old William very readily taking the bass-viol from its accustomed nail, and touching the strings as irreligiously as could be desired.

The country-dance called the 'Triumph, or Follow my Lover', was the figure with which they opened. The tranter took for his partner Mrs Penny, and Mrs Dewy was chosen by Mr Penny, who made so much of his limited height by a judicious carriage of the head, straightening of the back, and important flashes of his spectacle-glasses, that he seemed almost as tall as the tranter. Mr Shiner, age about thirty-five, farmer and churchwarden ... had come quite willingly to the party, and showed a wondrous obliviousness of all his antics on the previous night. But the comely, slender, prettily dressed prize Fancy Day fell to Dick's lot, in spite of some private machinations of the farmer, for the reason that Mr Shiner, as a richer man, had shown too much assurance in asking the favour, whilst Dick had been duly courteous.

[...] And so the dance proceeded. Mr Shiner, according to the interesting rule laid down, deserted his own partner and made off down the middle with this fair one of Dick's – the pair appearing from the top of the room like two persons tripping down a lane to be married. Dick trotted behind with what was intended to be a look of composure, but which was, in fact,

139

a rather silly expression of feature – implying, with too much earnestness, that such an elopement could not be tolerated. Then they turned and came back, when Dick grew more rigid around his mouth, and blushed with ingenuous ardour as he joined hands with the rival and formed the arch over his lady's head, which presumably gave the figure its name; relinquishing her again at setting to partners, when Mr Shiner's new chain quivered in every link, and all the loose flesh upon the tranter – who here came into action again – shook like jelly. Mrs Penny, being always rather concerned for her personal safety when she danced with the tranter, fixed her face to a chronic smile of timidity the whole time it lasted – a peculiarity which filled her features with wrinkles, and reduced her eyes to little straight lines like hyphens, as she jigged up and down opposite him; repeating in her own person not only his proper movements, but also the minor flourishes which the richness of the tranter's imagination led him to introduce from time to time – an imitation which had about it something of slavish obedience, not unmixed with fear.

[...] Minute after minute glided by, and the party reached the period when ladies' back-hair begins to look forgotten and dissipated; when

An old country dance.

a perceptible dampness makes itself apparent upon the faces even of delicate girls – a ghastly dew having for some time rained from the features of their masculine partners; when skirts begin to be torn out of their gathers; when elderly people, who have stood up to please their juniors, begin to feel sundry small tremblings in the region of the knees; when (at country parties of the thorough sort) waistcoats begin to be unbuttoned, and when the fiddlers' chairs have been wriggled, by the frantic bowing of their occupiers, to a distance of about two feet from where they originally stood.

Fancy was dancing with Mr Shiner. Dick knew that Fancy, by the law of good manners, was bound to dance as pleasantly with one partner as with another; yet he could not help suggesting to himself that she need not have put *quite* so much spirit into her steps, nor smiled *quite* so frequently whilst in the farmer's hands.

'I'm afraid you didn't cast off,' said Dick mildly to Mr Shiner, before the latter man's watch-chain had done vibrating from a recent whirl.

Fancy made a motion of accepting the correction; but her partner took no notice, and proceeded with the next movement with an affectionate bend towards her.

'That Shiner's too fond of her,' the young man said to himself as he watched them. They came to the top again, Fancy smiling warmly towards her partner, and went off to their places.

'Mr Shiner, you didn't cast off,' said Dick, for want of something else to demolish him with; casting off himself, and being put out at the farmer's irregularity.

'Perhaps I shan't cast off for any man,' said Mr Shiner.

'I think you ought to, sir.'

Dick's partner, a young lady of the name of Lizzy ... tried to mollify. 'I can't say that I myself have much feeling for casting off,' she said.

'Nor I,' said Mrs Penny, following up the argument; 'especially if a friend and neighbour is set against it. Not but that 'tis a terrible tasty thing in good hands and well done; yes, indeed, so say I.'

'All I meant was,' said Dick, rather sorry that he had spoken correctingly to a guest, 'that 'tis in the dance; and a man has hardly any right to hack and mangle what was ordained by the regular dance-maker, who, I daresay, got his living by making 'em, and thought of nothing else all his life.'

'I don't like casting off: then very well; I cast off for no dance-maker that ever lived.'

Dick now appeared to be doing mental arithmetic, the act being really an effort to present to himself, in an abstract form. How far an argument with a formidable rival ought to be carried when that rival was his mother's guest. The deadlock was put an end to by the stamping arrival up the middle of the tranter, who, despising minutiae on principle, started a theme of his own.

'I assure you, neighbours,' he said, 'the heat of my frame no tongue can tell!' He looked around and endeavoured to give, by a forcible gaze of self-sympathy, some faint idea of the truth.

Mrs Dewy formed one of the next couple.

'Yes,' she said in an auxiliary tone, 'Reuben always was such a hot man.'

Mrs Penny implied the species of sympathy that such a class of afliction required by trying to smile and look grieved at the same time.

'If he only walk round the garden of a Sunday morning his shirt-collar is as limp as no starch at all, continued Mrs Dewy, her countenance lapsing parenthetically into a housewifely expression of concern at the reminiscence.

'Come, come, you women-folk; 'tis hands-across – come, come!' said the tranter; and the conversation ceased for the present.

[...] Dick had at length secured Fancy for that most delightful of country-dances, opening with six-hands round.

'Before we begin,' said the tranter, 'my proposal is, that 'twould be a right and proper plan for every mortal man in the dance to pull off his jacket, considering the heat.'

'Such low notions as you have, Reuben! Nothing but strip will go down with you when you are a-dancing. Such a hot man as he is!'

[...] Dick, fearing to lose ground in Fancy's good opinion, retained his coat like the rest of the thinner men; and Mr Shiner did the same from superior knowledge.

And now a further phase of revelry had disclosed itself. It was the time of night when a guest may write his name in the dust upon the tables and chairs, and a bluish mist pervades the atmosphere, becoming a distinct halo round the candles... When the very fiddlers as well as the dancers get red in the face ... the fiddlers no longer sit down, but kick back their chairs and saw madly at the strings with legs firmly spread and eyes closed, regardless of the visible world. Again and again did Dick share his Love's hand with another man, and wheel round; then more delightfully, promenade in a circle with her all to himself, his arm holding her waist more firmly each time, and his elbow getting further and further behind her back, till the distance reached was rather noticeable; and, most blissful, swinging to places shoulder to shoulder, her breath curling round his neck like a summer zephyr that had strayed from its proper date. Threading the couples one by one they reached the bottom, when there arose in Dick's mind a minor misery lest the tune should end before they could work their way to the top again, and have anew the same exciting run down through. Dick's feelings on actually reaching the top in spite of his doubts were supplemented by a mortal fear that the fiddling might even stop at this supreme moment; which prompted him to convey a stealthy whisper to the far-gone musicians to the effect that they were not to leave off till he and his partner had reached the bottom of the dance once more, which remark was replied to by the nearest of those convulsed and quivering men by a private nod to the anxious young man between two semiquavers of the tune, and a simultaneous 'All right, ay, ay,' without opening the eyes. Fancy was now held so closely that Dick and she were practically one person. The room became to Dick like a picture in a dream, all that he could remember of it afterwards being the look of the fiddlers going to sleep as humming-tops sleep, by increasing their motion and hum together with the figures of grandfather James and old Simon Crumpler sitting by the chimney-corner talking and nodding in dumb-show, and beating the air to their emphatic sentences like people near a threshing machine.

The dance ended. 'Piph-h-h-h!' said tranter Dewy, blowing out his breath in the very finest stream of vapour that a man's lips could form. 'A regular tightener, that one, sonnies!' He wiped his forehead, and went to the cider and ale mugs on the table.

'Well!' Said Mrs Penny, flopping into a chair, 'my heart haven't been in such a thumping state of uproar since I used to sit up on old Midsummer Eves to see who my husband was going to be ... And a thing I never expected would come to pass ... Ah, the first spirit ever I see on a Midsummer Eve was a puzzle to me when he appeared, a hard puzzle, so say I!'

'So I should have fancied,' said Elias Spinks.

'Yes,' said Mrs Penny, 'never was I in such a taking as on that Midsummer Eve! I sat up, quite determined to see if John Wildway was going to marry me or no. I put the bread-and-cheese and beer quite ready, as the witch's book ordered, and I opened the door, and I waited till the clock struck twelve, my nerves all alive and so strained that

I could feel every one of 'em twitching like bell-wires. Yes, sure! And when the clock had struck, lo and behold I could see through the door a *little small* man in the lane wi' a shoemaker's apron on.'

Here Mr Penny stealthily enlarged himself half an inch.

'Now, John Wildway,' Mrs Penny continued, 'who courted me at that time, was a shoe-maker, you see, but he was a very fair-sized man, and I could't believe that any such a little man had anything to do wi' me, as anybody might. But on he came, and crossed the threshold – not John, but actually the same little small man in the shoemaker's apron –'

'You needn't be so mighty particular about little and small!' said her husband.

'In he walks, and down he sits, and O my goodness me, didn't I flee upstairs, body and soul hardly hanging together! Well, to cut a long story short, by-long and by-late John Wildway and I had a miff and parted; and lo and behold, the coming man came! Penny asked me if I'd go snacks with him, and afore I knew what I was about a'most, the thing was done.'

'I've fancied you never knew better in your life; but I mid be mistaken,' said Mr Penny in a murmur.

Thomas Hardy.

Christmas in the Workhouse
From the Dorset County Chronicle, *1862*

As the Victorian age progressed, the old medieval idea of Christmas as an extended season of goodwill, feasting and happiness was reintroduced into the community via the royal family and in 1847 the Poor Law Board, which had succeeded the Commissioners, ordered that Christmas dinner for the inmates of the workhouse should be an annual event. By the end of the nineteenth century, workhouses were everywhere decorated with greenery, a tree set up and benefactors invited to the Christmas dinner, which included beef or turkey and plum pudding with little presents given to the inmates — tobacco was a popular gift for the men. It was usual to have a simple entertainment after the Christmas tea — songs or carols by the inmates or those employed in the workhouse, and occasionally a magic lantern show.

The Dorset County Chronicle *reported two dinners for the inmates of the Dorchester Union in 1862, one on St Thomas's Day provided by the vicar and the other on Christmas Day itself provided by the Guardians, plus Boxing Day presents from a member of the local gentry.*

On St Thomas Day the aged inmates were entertained at the Grammar School by the Chaplain, the Rev. T. R. Maskew, according to his usual

custom, with a plentiful supply of roast beef and plum-pudding; while on Christmas Day the Guardians supplied every inmate of the house with a similar meal, besides a pint of ale to each person, and tobacco for the men. On the following day the whole of the inmates were provided with presents, to suit the tastes of all by E.L. Kindersley, Esq., of Syward Lodge.

A number of Unions doubled as lunatic asylums. In December 1903 the Dorset County Chronicle and Somersetshire Gazette *reported on the fortnightly meeting of the Dorchester Union Board of Guardians during which they discussed the recent visit of the Commissioner in Lunacy to the workhouse and reported that of the ninety-seven workhouse inmates, fifteen were classed as lunatics.*

There were 15 (insane) inmates in the house, 1 male and 14 female and all were properly detained. They looked well and were well cared for. Since the last visit 2 infirmary wards had been added, a new steam cooking apparatus had been placed in the kitchen and the house had been supplied with hot water, also new baths.

After Christmas 1831, Bridport Workhouse was without a Master and Matron. In January 1832, the Guardians advertised in the Dorset County Chronicle *for a married couple to function as managers of the Union:*

Wanted, for the Parish and Borough of Bridport, in the County of Dorset, a Man and his Wife, without Incumbrance, to execute the Duties of Assistant Overseer and Managers of the Poor-House. The Election will take place on or about the 1st of March next. Security to the amount of £300 will be required, with satisfactory Testimonials and references for Character.

Apply (if by letter, post-paid) to the Churchwardens and Overseers of Bridport.

N.B. No Persons need apply who reside within ten miles of Bridport.

Christmas Charities at Bere Regis and Blandford

*

St Thomas's Day (21 December) and Christmas Day were favoured times for charitable distributions of money and food to the poor of the parish. John Udal published the following account of Dorset's St Thomas's Day doleing:

A few days before Christmas, the women, children and old men in a parish would visit by turn the houses of their wealthier neighbours, and in return for and in recognition of Christmas greetings and their general demand of 'Please, give me something to keep a Christmas' (or 'for keeping up o' Christmas') would receive substantial pieces or 'hunks' of bread and cheese, bread and meat, or small sums of money. The old and infirm of either sex were generally represented by their children or grandchildren, those only being refused the dole who did not belong to the parish.

In the Middle Ages, many citizens left money to be invested or land to be used to provide an income for such charitable services for the good of their souls and remission of time in purgatory. Even after the Reformation such endowments continued. One such was created by the will of Jane Williams at the beautiful church of Bere Regis with its Turberville vaults, tombs and window. Thomas Hardy featured the church in his novel Tess of the d'Urbervilles, *where the Turbervilles feature as d'Urbervilles.*

Hutchins' History and Antiquities of Dorset gives a list for St John Baptist Church, Bere Regis, audited in October 1786, which includes several donations of £5

or £10 'In money, the use thereof to be given to the poor yearly on St Thomas'. The donators include 'Matthew Turberville, gent' and 'John Turberville, esq.' An indenture of 1830 in Hutchins', also for Dorset, lists dividends to be distributed by the vicar:

on Christmas-day, or between that day and the 1st of January, yearly, between two men and two women of the most deserving poor inhabitants of the parish of Bere Regis... The vicar distributes the dividends at Christmas, between two poor men and two poor women, fifty shillings each, and the objects of the charity have been changed every year.'

By the Victorian period, self-help was encouraged with clothing clubs, where charity was added to existing and proven thrift. A club recorded in 1843 at Blandford by the Commission on the Employment of Women and Children in Agriculture encouraged membership from 'Any labouring family of good conduct'. Subscription was a penny and thruppence a week. At Christmas 'these subscriptions are doubled by the donations of persons in a better position of life living in the neighbourhood'. The club members had to spend the money at the shop of 'the tradesman appointed to supply the club', the purchases having to be 'plain articles of dress or household linen'. It was 'an imperative rule of the club that if any subscriber purchases with club-money any articles of dress or linen not of a plain and useful description, he ceases to be a member. There were two thousand pounds' worth of purchases by this club during the Christmas period 1843.

St John Baptist Church, Bere Regis, from Hutchins' *History and Antiquities of Dorset*.

Christmas Earthquake at Lyme Regis

'The Mighty Landslip' by Laurence Dopson
From the Dorset County Journal, 1947

✳

The famous blue lias cliffs of Lyme Regis, with their sandstone coverings, are notoriously friable and have produced many landslips. The most famous and substantial of these in recorded history was that on Christmas Day 1839, when about forty acres collapsed about three miles to the west of Lyme Regis, which opened a chasm a mile long and 400ft wide in places. This triggered the changing of the coastline between Lyme Regis and the estuary of the River Axe, the result being the National Nature Reserve of the Undercliff.

Laurence Dopson's article begins by talking generally about the problems of a number of landslips in the Lyme area and then specifically deals with the dramatic events of Christmas Day 1839, incorporating contemporary local accounts, including that of the Lyme Regis historian Dr Roberts. The farm labourer William Critchard seem to have had a particularly kind and attentive employer in Farmer Chappell, who had built him a new cottage shortly before the landslip and sent down his waggon to help the evacuation.

Also, on the night before the main landslip – Christmas Eve – the Critchards were celebrating Christmas with their employer from sunset until one in the morning, including dinner. The celebration was connected with the ashen faggot and as this is normally reckoned to be a Somerset and Devon celebration, it is interesting to find this record of it on the Dorset border. The ash tree seems to have had magical connotations in Anglo-Saxon pagan culture connected with Yuletide

An ashen
faggot
ceremony.

*and the solstice, and these survived into the Christmas period where, in the west
of England, faggots of young ash saplings bound with withies or osiers formed the
basis of the Christmas fire; between five and nine bonds are recorded.*
C.H. Poole in The Customs, Superstitions and Legends of the County
of Somerset *(1977) records interesting details, including the breaking down of
status and an ingenious Christian connection:*

The faggot is composed of ashen sticks, hooped round with bands of
the same tree, nine in number. When placed on the fire, fun and jollity
commence – master and servant are now all at equal footing. Sports
begin – jumping in sacks, diving in the water for apples, and many other
innocent games engage the attention of the rustics. Every time the bands
crack by reason of the heat of the fire, all present are supposed to drink
liberally of cider or egg-hot, a mixture of cider, eggs, etc. The reason why

ash is selected in preference to any other timber is that tradition assigns it as the wood with which Our Lady kindled a fire in order to wash her new-born Son.

In some areas the bursting of the withies was connected to solstitial divination practices, such as prognostication of success in love. In one Somerset account, engaged couples each selected a withy and they would be said to marry in the order of the bursting of the withies. In Dorset, 'even' ash leaves (those lacking a terminal leaflet and therefore having an even number of leaflets) were used for divination. John Udal in his Dorsetshire Folk-Lore *says:*

The ash leaf is frequently invoked by young girls as a matrimonial oracle in the following way: The girl who wishes to divine who her future lover or husband is to be plucks an even ash leaf, and holding it in her hand, says:

> The even ash leaf in my hand,
> The first I meet shall be my man.

Then putting it into her glove, adds:

> The even ash leaf in my glove,
> The first I meet shall be my love.

And lastly, into her bosom, saying:

> The even ash leaf in my bosom,
> The first I meet shall be my husband.

Soon after which the future lover or husband will be sure to make his appearance.

A vivid memory of Dorset 40 years ago is the end of a coffin protruding over the shore where Church Cliff, Lyme Regis, had fallen away. This part of Dorset, and as far along the coast into Devon as Branscombe and Sidmouth, has frequently been the scene of landslips and other phenomena connected with rock movement. There were big slips on the Isle of Portland, for instance, in the 17th cebnury and in 1734 and 1792, and a so-called 'earthquake' at Lyme in 1689.

''Tis the lias,' an old man once explained to me. But it is not only the lias. The greensand also is treacherous. In 1825, old Mr John Warren warned his fellow commissioners of the turnpike that their proposed deep cutting in the greensand between Lyme and Charmouth would be unsuccessful, the whole of that elevated valley having subsided forty years earlier. They ignored him, had the cutting made – and three years later, in January, 1828, the road slipped down towards the sea from twenty feet at one end to eight feet at the other, though admittedly it was not until 26th May, 1924, that the road had finally to be closed.

A waterspout passing low over the land near Gabriel's, between Golden Cap and Shorne Cliff, is believed to have caused the big slip here about 1724. Heavy rains frequently bring trouble. Sudden rains following very hot weather in August, 1751, caused the lias cliffs between Lyme and Charmouth literally to catch fire and local people will remember seeing this happen again at the beginning of the present century. The memorable wet season of 1764 was followed by a slip at Whitlands, just west of Lyme. It is therefore not surprising that in 1839, when, according to the Engineer of the Southampton railway, more rain fell than ever before in living memory, the biggest subsidence of all should occur.

[...] It rained nearly every day during that summer of 1839. And the rain continued all through the autumn and into the winter. About a fortnight before Christmas, labourers at Dowland's Farm, three miles west of Lyme, observed a slight settlement of the undercliff there. They remarked about it but did not take much notice, as strange movements of the land were fairly common hereabouts.

On the Monday before Christmas Day, 1839, William Critchard, one of the labourers who lived on the Undercliff at Dowlands, noticed that the plastering of his cottage was cracking and the door jammed, but as the house had not been built above two years he dismissed these occurrences as being due to ordinary settling. Next day, 24th December, he went to his work at 6 a.m. As usual but did not return at sundown as his wife joined him and the other farm-hands and their wives, to burn the ashen faggot at Dowlands farm house. They all sat round Farmer Chappell's fireside, probably in the room looking out at the old farm bell and the yard, the same room in which I enjoyed many Christmas parties a hundred years later. They had supper and talked and emptied their tankards every time one of the bonds of the faggot burst in the flames.

It was one o'clock on Christmas morning before the party broke up and Mr and Mrs Critchard made their way across the barton and over the fields to their home. William did not notice as they drew near that the path had subsided one foot since his ascent 19 hours before, nor was he in a state to feel worried when the mother who had been looking after the children said she was alarmed, and so were the neighbours, at mysterious crackings. "Tis as if something be coming upon us,' she remonstrated, but Mr and Mrs Critchard just went to bed. At four o'clock, however, William was roused by an extra loud crack; by five he said he could bide no longer. What happened next is best described in the dramatic narrative of Dr Roberts:

> Critchard rose and found the garden had large fissures in it. He used a stick to open the door, got out and called to his neighbours

that the house was going. His neighbour began to take down a new clock, but a joist had settled upon it which prevented him, until great force was used in raising the joist. The land continued cracking all the while. Between six and seven on Christmas morning, their little household goods being out, he went up to tell his master what had occurred. The land had then settled down by the upper cliff seven feet, and he had to climb up. Farmer Chappell sent down a waggon to remove the furniture; and the labourers had here and there to repair the road to enable this loaded vehicle to proceed.

But worse was to come. The next night – Christmas night – two Preventive men, James Robertson and his companion, were walking over the cliff path from Axmouth to the coastguard station at Whitlands, when Robertson stumbled across a slight ridge of gravel, 'which at first they thought only the work of mischevious boys,' reports the Rev. W. D. Conybeare in his *Memoir and Views of Dowlands Landslip*. Soon, however, one of them jammed his foot in a fissure. It being the twentieth of the moon, they could now see great fissures opening and closing around them. It must have been a terrifying experience, for at any moment the earth might have opened beneath the feet of the two men and that would have been the end. And these strange movements were taking place in silence, save for a sound like the rending of cloth as the land split – and the wind, which now increased in violence.

Robertson was going to his guard. Spencer and Johns were on their's at Culverhole beach. A little after midnight these men were alarmed to observe a boiling of the sea at Dowlands as the sea-bed 10 feet below high water mark was forced bodily upwards to form a raised beach or reef 40 feet high above the water; for days to come this was to be the scene of feasting as hundreds of crows consumed the limpets, periwinkles and crabs. Nor was this all the three men saw that Christmas night. They watched, amazed, as the familiar outline of the cliffs changed, the shore altered and a deep chasm was formed. The attrition of chert flints as the 8,000,000 tons of earth subsided gave rise to eerie flashings and a smell as of sulphur. A few weeks later, on 3rd February, 1840, as a result of the continued heavy rains of January, a similar slip took place at Whitlands, on the Dorset side. Early in the morning the coastguard cottages tilted at an alarming angle, but the tenants escaped. Later, the end of the cottages towards the high ground was depressed, 'and soon after, as the hollow filled with water became flooded, the upper storey alone appeared out of the lake'.

Dowlands Landslip just after its occurrence was even more impressive than it is now, since its naked grandeur appeared fresh and unobscured by luxuriant vegetation. One person who came to see it from Honiton was so overawed that he was taken home to a sick bed, from which he recovered with difficulty. A sculptor who journeyed from London to make a model of the slip desisted when he saw how extensive it was. The undercliff 'made Bishop Atterbury break out into language expressive of the greatest admiration' and two Ashantee princes came to view it. An inevitable pamphlet appeared saying the whole thing had been prophesied in Revelations (xi, 13). Relatives tried hard to dissuade a lady from taking a holiday in Lyme, because, they said, she might get swallowed up in the earth.

A charge of 6d per head was soon made for persons wishing to view the slip – and the charge remains 6d per head to this day. One of the cottages was completely destroyed, the other appeared intact at first sight, but upon closer examination the foundations were found to have sunk a foot, whilst the lime floors had been squeezed upwards and the

Landslip cottage.

doorposts and window frames buckled by pressure. The outlines of the original cottages can still be seen and stones from them were used in building the present one. I remember the difficulty we had to take a coffin up the narrow cliff path to the top, when a person died down there. People visiting the landslip a hundred and seven years ago were provided with refreshments by Mrs Critchard.

The Darkling Thrush
By Thomas Hardy

Thomas Hardy published this poem in the Graphic *on 29 December 1900, under the title 'By the Century's Deathbed' and added the date '31 December 1900' at the foot to indicate that this poem was ushering out the old century and welcoming in the new (the century beginning in 1901, just as the new millenium should have been celebrated in 2001!) The poem was published in Hardy's collection of poetry* Poems of the Past and the Present *in 1901.*

Thomas Hardy and Emma at Max Gate, *c.* 1900.

I leant upon a coppice gate
When Frost was spectre-gray,
And Winter's dregs made desolate
The weakening eye of day.
The tangled bine-stems scored the sky
Like strings of broken lyres,
And all mankind that haunted nigh
Had sought their household fires.

The land's sharp features seemed to be
The Century's corpse outleant,
His crypt the cloudy canopy,
The wind his death-lament.
The ancient pulse of germ and birth
Was shrunken hard and dry,
And every spirit upon earth
Seemed fervourless as I.

At once a voice arose among
The bleak twigs overhead
In a full-hearted evensong
Of joy illimited;
An aged thrush, frail, gaunt, and small,
In blast-beruffled plume,
Had chosen thus to fling his soul
Upon the growing gloom.

So little cause for carolings
Of such ecstatic sound
Was written on terrestrial things
Afar or nigh around,
That I could think there trembled through
His happy good-night air
Some blessed Hope, whereof he knew
And I was unaware.

Christmas in the County Hospital, 1913

From the Somersetshire Gazette, 1 January 1914

✳

This account of how Christmas was spent in the quiet well-run wards of the Dorset County Hospital in 1913 inadvertently reflects the stable and traditionalist world of the Edwardian period. No one could know at that point that they were on the very brink of a world war where death tolls and casualties would be on a scale undreamed of in world history.

'Nothing new' might be the cynic's observation on the keeping of Christmas in Dorchester. Our rejoinder is as apt as it is brief – 'Happily!' For the essence of felicity at this festive season is found in doglike fidelity to the tender tradition and appealing associations of the past.

Thus the assumption that there was 'nothing new' in our observation, sacred and social, of the great Feast of the Nativity, grafted on to the stock of Saxon Yuletide, is the best compliment that could be paid, the greatest assurance that the Dorchester Christmastide was well nigh all that a Christmastide should be. Had we not the frosty air, so fine a medium for the transportation of the dulcet melody of Christmas bells? Had we not the midnight waits and the carollers, the holly-decked churches, the fireside family reunions, the old-fashioned festive fare, the opening of the hand of philanthropy so fit at a season of goodwill towards men, especially the poor, the needy, the afflicted?

We indicate below ... the happy way in which Christmas was spent at the Dorset County Hospital.

A nurse's uniform, 1897.

At The County Hospital

Again, as far as physical suffering and disability and absence from the home would admit, Christmas day was a day of peaceful happiness for the patients of the Dorset County Hospital. Acting in the spirit of the institution's motto, Christo in pauperibus, thoughtful and charitable people had contributed liberally in money and in 'kind' to the Christmas bounty so freely dispersed within the grey walls: and the Matron (Miss Cotton) and the Acting House Surgeon (Dr Bevil Collard) and the whole staff did their utmost to shed beams of festive happiness on the patients this time thirty-one in number.

Charming Decorations

A good supply of holly and evergreens had been sent by Mr H.B. Middleton of Bradford Peverell, Mr G.W. Floyer of Stafford, and the Rev. John G. Brymer of Puddletown, and with these and other materials,

A typical cot in the children's ward, 1878.

the nurses were busy all day Wednesday decorating the wards and corridors, the work of their nimble fingers, the sundry deft touches being watched with interest and pleasure by the patients lying abed. For be it remembered, a large share of the pleasure of life is pleasure of anticipation, of expectation.

In the male wards the prevailing tones of colour were rich yellow and dark green. All the lamps were shaded with yellow and dark green crinkled paper. The central object in the main ward was a wonderful prize 'dip' which Sister Hughes had made in the shape of a monstrous cracker.

Upstairs, under Sister Smith's supervisions, the female ward was decorated in pink and white, the dark polished green of foliage being picked out daintily with pink roses... Moreover, to be in harmony with the surroundings the patients were proudly wearing pink bed-jackets, made by the Sisters, whose handiwork, pleasant to the eyes as well as materially warming, was received with grateful thanks. The small children's ward is a corner of the hospital to which one always turns with special tenderness. There were fewer little folk in cots than usual. They were wearing light blue bed jackets: and Santa Claus was especially bountiful towards them – gentle hearted Old Fellow! – they were supremely happy with dolls and soldiers and kitchen ranges... The corridors too had received attention and been brightened with Chinese lanterns and evergreen.

The Celebration

Quite properly, the celebration was not postponed until Christmas morning, but opened on Christmas eve, with the procession of nurses, who, carrying candles, went round to the wards in the good old fashioned style singing carols, to the piano accompaniments played by Nurse Minney. As the lights in the wards were all turned down, the effect both phonetic and dramatic, was most pleasing. The friends of the hospital had responded so liberally to the appeal sent out by the Matron and as a result every patient received a substantial parcel of useful garments, besides pretty things for themselves and their families. Each man was given a really good shirt, and the women night gowns, as well as books and knick-knacks. The children and some of the women kept up the habits of childhood by hanging up their stockings.

[...] At nine-thirty on Christmas morning, there was a service in the beautiful little chapel which bye the bye possesses one of the most artistic window to be found in Dorchester, representing Christ as Consolator, and Shepherd. The interior had been decorated by Sister Pickett and her night nurse.

The Christmas Dinner

At the early hour of noon, the Christmas dinner was served in the wards... Roast turkey, with vegetables was followed by the indispensable plum pudding, and then there was quite a variety of sweets in the way of jellies, blancmanges and custards. The Matron carved for the men and the like duty was performed in the women's ward by the visiting Home Surgeon. This excellent dinner was followed by dessert and crackers and a whiff of tobacco for those who cared for it, the wherewithal being provided by Dr Collard.

Zitten Out the Wold Year
By William Barnes

✳

The celebration of New Year was more important as a secular and social activity even than Christmas Day in nineteenth-century Dorset. This is another of William Barnes' vivid dialect poems.

Why, rain or sheen, or blow or snow,
I zaid, if I could stand so's,
I'd come, vor all a friend or foe,
To sheake ye by the hand, so's;
An' spend, wi' kinsvo'k near an'dear,
A happy evenen, woonce a year,
A-zot wi' me'th
Avore the he'th
To zee the new year in, so's.

There's Jim an' Tom, a-grown the size
O' men, girt lusty chaps, so's,
An' Fanny wi' her sloo-black eyes,
Her mother's very daps, so's;
An' little Bill, so brown's a nut,
An' Poll, a gigglen little slut,
I hope will shoot
Another voot
The year that's comen in, so's.

165

An' there, upon his mother's knee,
So peart do look about, so's,
The little woone ov all, to zee
His vu'st wold year goo out, so's.
An' zoo mid God bless all o's still,
Gwain up or down along the hill,
To meet in glee
Agean to zee
A happy new year in, so's.

The wold clock's han' do softly steal
Up roun' the year's last hour, so's;
Zoo let the han'-bells ring a peal,
Lik' them a-hung in tow'r, so's.
Here, here be two vor Tom, an' two
Vor Fanny, an' a peair vor you;
We'll meake em swing,
An' meake em ring,
The merry new year in, so's.

Tom, mind your time there; you be wrong.
Come let your bells all sound, so's:
A little clwoser, Poll; ding, dong!
There, now 'tis right all round, so's.
The clock's a-striken twelve, d'ye hear?
Ting, ting, ding, dong! Farewell, wold year!
'Tis gone, 'tis gone! –
Goo on, goo on,
An' ring the new woone in, so's!

Sherborne Christmas Ball

From the Dorset County Chronicle, *1832*

A highly stylised and pseudo-literary piece of journalism from the days when journalists were expected to be cultured and well-versed in poetry. Surprisingly little is actually told us about the ball, however!

> Methinkes I hear, methinkes I see
> Sweet musicke, wondrous melodie
> Rare beauties, gallant ladies shine,
> Whate'er is lovely or divine
> To dancing other joys are folly,
> Away, away with melancholy
> (Old Ballad)

On Friday last, was held at the Town-Hall in Sherborne, the Annual Christmas Ball, the brilliance of which was only to be exceeded by the spirit and animation of the dancing. The room, painted for the occasion a subdued salmon colour, was tastefully decorated with festoons of laurels interspersed with mirrors, reflecting the dazzling tapers' light 'in numbers numberless'. At the upper end was an antique screen, with crimson chintz hangings ... The scene was altogether of antique beauty, and it seemed as if one of Genii had waved his magic wand, and produced an Arabian night's entertainment. About nine o'clock, carriages, freighted with youth and beauty, rolled along the streets in quick succession from all directions and shortly after that hour Upjohn's Band (which was in attendance from Weymouth) struck up a lively quadrille. The sound, like the call of balmy Spring on the feathered tribe, produced a general flutter and ruffling of plumes, and it became evident that 'pairing season' had arrived – numberless were the little gallantries and delicate attentions of the enraptured partners as they figured through the evolutions of each quadrille:

> Nods, and becks, and wreathed smiles,
> Such as hang on Hebe's cheek,
> Or love to live in dimples sleek

The scene was occasionally diversified by the graceful waltz, which, whatever certain antiquated spinsters may declare to the contrary,

Above: A couple enjoy a dance together.
Right: Sheet music for a quadrille.

has certainly a moral tendency – it teaches the necessity of every couple pulling together, and the benefits of mutual support in the whirligig of life. Anon, they scampered through the lively gallopede and 'shuffled off their mortal coil', moving, as it were, with no earthly step. Indeed, it was altogether a goodly sight. Several gentlemen from distant countries, remarked that they had never seen a richer display of beauty, and fastidious indeed, must have been the taste that could not here be gratified. Here was loveliness in all its varieties – the sweet Madonna countenance, a painter's study, with raven hair, and large dark dreamy eyes, curtained with silken fringes – fair maids, with cheeks like alabaster tinged with nature's rosy red – the stately dignity of the Roman matron; or the classic elegance of The Grecian Helen, 'whose matchless features set the world on fire' – the miniature symmetry of the Medici school; or lofty ladies, in 'lengthened sweetness long drawn out' – all, all were here. In short, there was every style and variety of female loveliness, so that in the language of the most voluptuous of modern poets, it might be said:

> If ever there was an Elysium on Earth,
> It was this! It was this!

Great credit is due to the Stewards for their unremitting exertions and attention to the company; and despite of the cant which will discourage such innocent festivities, a general determination was expressed to patronise them at the returning season next year. Certainly no amusement can be more rational than that which brings families together, and keeps up friendly feelings and good neighbourhood; particularly in these days, when political strife and puritanical gloom darken the horizon, and seem eager to wither the social charities of life.

Christmas in Wartime
From the Southern Times, *1939*

Dorset, along with the rest of the country, was at war in 1939, and this article shows how the women of Dorset were courageously coping with Christmas without menfolk and with the newly introduced food and petrol rationing, as well as the evacuees.

The blacker it is outside the brighter will be our hearths and the Englishman's home being traditionally his castle, everyone will be settled down to a Christmas with as much or more festivity than usual.

Everything should be done to change the appearances of our rooms at this season, but it should be done as tastefully as possible. A few sprigs of holly or – since holly is usually difficult to get – hips and haws varnished bright red look better than a mass of paper hangings which get in the way, are too easily set on fire, and look very tawdry in the sunlight of a Boxing Day morning.

Don't forget the mistletoe, but don't put it in the dining room – the hall is the place – and as the hall is often a cold place (at least after a good warm dinner and a little of 'something') it will keep your guests sociable, give them just enough to stimulate their appetite, before they realise that it's decidedly chilly out there. Christmas may be traditionally a Bacchanalia, but keep it sociable!

But the *sine qua non* is availability of nuts, raisins, chocolates and intriguing sweets placed in strategically opportune places where your guests can come on them by surprise, as it were, and nibble without ostentation, it will be as well to get a stock of these delicacies in now – and don't forget the crystallised fruits, figs and dates which go down as well with the children today as they did with their fathers.

Christmas too is a good time to replace your emergency food store – tinned meat, soups, coffee … sardines, prawns – which have probably been on the shelf for some months. Extras such as jellies, blancmanges and biscuits should be laid in as large a stock as possible for those unexpected arrivals who appear at the holiday season.

Don't forget your aspirin for even the most abstemious tends to feel the strain on Boxing Day and New Year morning.

This Christmas, even more than previous ones, will be an 'at home' season though if you want to go out by car and have wangled extra petrol, you will find a full moon to accommodate your way.

See that your wireless set is in perfect order, and your funds run to get new records. Nearly every party ends with an impromptu dance and you will want to try out steps of the 'Siegfried' walk which are quite enchanting in their lunacy. It is not advisable to have the radio going on at the background of a party unless the music is cheerful and ear tickling: otherwise it tends to split the crowd into groups who want to listen to Tommy Handley and those who want to play musical chairs – incompatible aims.

But however we spend our Christmas – whether quietly with one or two friends, or in a house party, or even working at our jobs – our thoughts will turn to those who are not lucky enough to be with us, those who in one way or another are making it possible for us to spend our Christmas according to our own ideas, rather than in some burrow beneath the ground. What are we going to send them that will be of most use to them at this time? Sweets and smokes are going to be in great demand, and a large variety is already available in all confectionery and tobacconist's shops.

Another new element this year will be the presence in many homes of evacuees. We have no need to give advice about kindliness to the English *hausfrau* upon this subject, and we do not need to shirk the psychological difficulties... Special attention should be given to these nomads who are in most cases spending their first Christmas away from their parents.

Christmas Comforts
From the Southern Times, *December 1939*

✳

In this brief article from the Southern Times, *we learn that the 2nd Dorsets were spending their first Christmas of the war away from home (at an unspecified location) and in obviously uncomfortable conditions when this letter was written by their commanding officer thanking the Dorset women's group, the Dorset Committee for Comfort for Dorset Forces, for their 'Christmas Comforts'.*

An example of good work being done by the Dorset Committee for Comfort for Dorset Forces is afforded by the following letter from Lieutenant Colonel E.L. Stephenson Commands 2nd Battalion Dorsetshire Regiment with the B.E.F. which has been received by Lieutenant Colonel J.V. Shute Hon Secretary and treasurer of the committee:

Dear Colonel Shute,

A parcel of socks &c … A list of which you sent me … has arrived safely today. I want to thank the Dorset Committee very much indeed for the comforts, which will be tremendously appreciated by the NCOs and men of the 2nd Battalion.

The weather has been very wet and icy and men are seldom able to dry their socks. Those of them who have gum boots wear holes in their socks extremely quickly. As the weather gets colder gloves and scarves will be particularly needed.

Will you please be kind enough to convey the thanks of all ranks of this Battalion to the Committee.

Yours very sincerely,

Signed E.L. Stephenson, Lt. Col.

Village Pantomime
By D. Cresswell

The Christmas or New Year pantomime, in less commercial days, was an important feature of village and small town life, helping to bind people together socially. Why this particular village pantomime was a 'one-off' is not explained until the last sentence!

Our village lay some 20 miles from a town large enough to boast a theatre and that Wonder of Wonders, the Christmas Pantomime: and as the only means of getting to the town in question consisted of two or three daily trains chugging sleepily along the branch line without the slightest connection or concern for theatre hours, Prue and I had to content ourselves with newspaper cuttings.

Then came a winter which brought a terrific surprise. Hurrying home from school on a frosty afternoon, to our amazement we saw that every large tree and every barn carried a huge, flaming poster announcing a 'Stupendous forthcoming Production of Cinderella' in the Village Hall. Prue and I goggled, then took to our heels and flew home to tell mother, who calmly replied that she 'knew all about it, she had bought tickets for the front row and we'd better behave ourselves or we wouldn't be going'; then she took up her sewing as though pantomimes in the Village Hall were a part of our daily round, instead of something that had never happened before.

Such a thing did not happen again, so I had better start from the beginning and tell the full story.

When Miss Matilda Williams reached her eighty-eighth birthday, she said, quite simply, 'that she'd had enough of this old world,' and a few weeks later took to her bed and died. So the house known as 'Red Tiles', tenanted by Miss Williams for over 50 years, stood empty and neglected. Until one day along came Mrs Camelia Spriggs, a thin, middle-aged woman who had become a widow three months before. The late Mr Spriggs had been a minor civil servant in the depths of Whitehall and he and his spouse had lived in a semi-detached house somewhere in that labyrinth known as Greater London, where they had devoted the whole of their spare time to the local Dramatic Club. Between them, Mr and Mrs Spriggs had 'produced' Shakespeare in large quantities, with Ibsen or Shaw thrown in to make a change. When Mr Spriggs died Camelia decided that her pension would 'go farther' in the country. And so Mrs Camelia Spriggs came to live in our midst.

In great spirits the good lady set out to call on every farm and cottage in the parish, urging one and all to join her 'Shakespeare Club'.

Apart from seasonal landwork and the meetings of the 'Monthly Club', the ladies of the village had no great diversions, and were ever on the lookout for a bit of distraction and fun. They invited Mrs Spriggs to attend the next 'Monthly Meeting' and there make the acquaintance of Mrs Maggie Monro, who 'managed' everything, but happened to be away for a few days just then.

Maggie Monro was in her fifties. She stood 5 feet 10 inches in her socks and turned the scales at 14 stone, but in spite of her bulk Maggie was not ungainly. She had neat ankles and feet, well-kept hands, small features, a kind mouth, and a pair of large, childish, forget-me-not blue eyes. Known for miles around as the life and soul of the party, Maggie couldn't bear things to be 'dull'. To 'liven things up a bit' she had begun her 'Club'.

Maggie Monro listened gravely to Mrs Spriggs' suggestions relating to the proposed 'Shakespeare Club', then she threw back her head and exploded with laughter.

'Wot us?' and Maggie roared again.

But soon Christmas came, and with it one of Maggie Monro's sailor sons home on leave. He gave his mother a special treat in the form of a visit to a pantomime in the nearby town. It was Maggie's first trip to such a performance and she was overcome with delight. She talked of the show all day long and dreamed of it during the night. Before the week was out she called on her 'Club' friends, insisting that one and all went to the pantomime. The coach set off fully loaded and before they returned home that night, Maggie Monro's mind was made up, the 'Club' should produce *Cinderella* in the parish hall.

Mrs Spriggs was completely overwhelmed to find that she was expected to produce a pantomime! Shakespeare, with perhaps Ibsen for a change, was one thing, but a pantomime! However, the 'Club' was in such a fervour of excitement that Mrs Spriggs threw her fears to the wind and determined to bring forth a pantomime worthy of her former efforts of play production.

To the credit of everyone, they worked hard, and so great was the demand for tickets that it was decided to run the show on two nights instead of only one.

Came the Great Night!

Maggie Monro set such a glorious example by romping heartily through her part as the leading 'ugly sister' that it was impossible for anyone else to lag behind, and a marvellous evening was had by both performers and audience.

Mrs Spriggs was most gratified, and Maggie Monro, quite drunk with success, determined to make the ensuing performance 'go' with even more gusto. She called the vicar's gardener and her fellow-actresses to a special and strictly private meeting early next morning.

The result of this meeting became known when *Cinderella* was well in its stride for the second time.

The Good Fairy appeared, waved her wand to produce the silver coach and hey presto! on to the stage trotted the wheelwright's Billy-goat harnessed to a small wooden truck. Both goat and truck were beautifully decorated, but alas, all the decorations in the world could not dim Billy's natural 'perfume'.

Billy let out a series of loud Maa-aa-aas and from the back of the hall came answering Maa-aas from children.

It was Billy's first stage appearance but evidently he liked his role, for he refused to leave at the Good Fairy's command, and ambled about the stage, making playful butts at Maggie Monro, when she tried to lead him away. The onlookers applauded loudly, until the wheelwright was called upon to leave his seat and conduct his amusing though smelly animal off the stage.

The performance rolled on to the scene of the ball. The dancing began; a graceful gavotte as on the previous night. And then the gramophone blared a resounding tune for a country dance. On to the stage swept Maggie Monro and the entire cast, dancing as they had never danced before!

The stage, none too steady from the very beginning, creaked and swayed.

Then suddenly, it happened! There was a terrific crash, a prolonged splintering and then, complete darkness; the latter pierced by loud shrieks and yells. The stage had collapsed.

The Dorset Ooser

*

The Ooser was a masked figure who appeared at Christmas and May Day festivities in the village of Melbury Osmond, sometimes with a retinue chasing women by the water splash in the centre of the village; this would give a fertility aspect to the figure and the name is possibly of Celtic derivation, being similar to a Celtic word meaning water. The name may have later acquired devilish

The Dorset Ooser, 1891.

connotations as there are also memories of lucifer matches being placed in the mask and lighted and chains being attached to give a demonic effect.

In the nineteenth century, the Ooser mask was owned by the Cave family at Holt Farm, Melbury Osmond, but lost when the family left the county. The mask was of wood with hair and horns and gnashing teeth and a moveable lower jaw operated by a string. There was a rounded boss between the eyebrows. At one time the Ooser mask was apparently kept in the Malt House and in Thomas Hardy's day in the church and he refers to it as being there in his collection of short stories A Group of Noble Dames; there is also a reference to the Ooser in The Return of the Native. William Barnes's Glossary of the Dorset Dialect *(1886) describes it as 'A mask with grim jaws, put on with a cow's skin to frighten folk'* and there is a photograph of the Melbury Osmond mask, together with some background information in Somerset and Dorset Notes and Queries *1891.*

The Ooser was not exclusive to Melbury. Hardy's friend Henry Moule remembered that 'In my childhood he was doing service – at Christmas mummings, surely it was. Our Cerne Abbas nurse was quite up in all relating to the 'wurser', as I should spell it phonetically.' There is a tradition of the Ooser at Shillingstone and a tin Ooser mask surviving in a museum at Lyme Regis and the Weymouth Morris men have revived the custom.

The Christmas Thrift Club
By John Edward

Winter

The long, golden days of St Martin's Little Summer go by, each night the mists gathering deeper along the valley-bottom behind the farm; each morning a few more brown leaves fluttering down from the chestnut trees that line the street to join the mounds of dead leaves in the fields – tiny pimpernel glowing scarlet in the stubble, the swathe-turning machine still, standing disconsolate and rusty in a corner of Lower Mead, the thatch of the corn ricks still fairly new and shiny. And then, suddenly, it is winter – black winter, overnight, with a great gale roaring in the swaying chestnuts and black clouds sweeping from the north, and rain spattering in sudden showers. In the evening, as the light gets duckish, the Manor Farm tractor come belching down through the village, its trailing laden with faggots (for the men have been wood-leazing up on Longdistance); and old Levi Cox, high atop the piled faggots, shouts: 'Winter's come at last!' And we know that this really is the end of the long Indian summer which followed so surprisingly the wet months of July and August.

So, here we are in the wintertime, in the deep heart of the Dorset countryside, the last visitors long gone from our byways and the shingle of the beach untrodden by their feet. Men assume an earth-stained timeless look from the wet and windy weather which colours their clothes and faces. Muddy gaiters, or 'yorks' tied beneath the knee of

A cottage
in the snow,
Colehill.

earthy corduroys, floppy, colourless hats, long jackets of stout greeny-
black tweed with deep poachers' pockets, now, alas, empty of rabbits
– but there is hope that the rabbits may come back, for two nights ago
I saw a young, healthy rabbit lollop over the road and crouch against
the hedge as in the old days. I mentioned this at the village pub, and
there was an immediate chorus: 'Yurr, now don't 'ee tell a soul where
you saw'n to – else some beggar 'ull have he.' The Christian feeling
against the big commercial farmers who introduced the dreadful scourge
of myxomatosis is very strong among farm labourers and small, local
farmers – it is not entirely a question of their having lost a staple article
of diet and income, but a matter of ordinary virtue and what Dorset
people call 'loving kindness' – however great a pest the rabbits were,
there had been no need to inflict such cold and deliberate torture on
small animals who, after all, were innocent in their fragile, rabbity life
about the fields and woodlands: after all *they* didn't know it was Farmer
So-and-so's young corn they were eating.

The Christmas Thrift Club

On the last Thursday before Christmas, the Christmas Thrift Club breaks. All year, men have been putting their weekly shillings and half-crowns into the Providence Inn Club Fund, and now they are suddenly rich; and early in the evening at the inn, there is a general air of determination to get fairly drunk tonight. George Merry already had out his melodion, and old Fritz his banjo, and the pints of rough cyder and beer come rapidly from the barrel-room while the first songs are bellowed out. 'Gi'e us Rock 'n Roll, Georger,' shouts a young tractor-driver; but George Merry knows nothing of such modern trumpery, and breaks immediately into one of the old village songs we all know and love, although they have been sung so many, many times over the past decades. 'Wire in, my lads', 'Buttercup Joe', 'The Burning Sands of Egypt', 'When the fields are white with daisies'; and then Levi Cox, the old, retired carrier, (his wife under the churchyard yew a year ago, his horses long gone to the knacker, and his passengers' descendants travelling now by the impersonal national bus) sings in a quavering voice:

> She went away a month today,
> Her absence grieves me greatly;
> With a strawberry mark upon her arm,
> O, have you seen her lately?

And now the sweet-voiced baker, and his rousing song about 'The Ship that Never Returned', and now Billy Coombe, 'best man i' the village', is on his feet, swaying violently and bellowing out his only song. Billy, blown up and buried alive on the Somme in 1916, has the lined, loyal face of the eternal English man-at-arms and his song was forgotten by everyone else long ago:

> The Whiz–Bang is the swiftest thing
> Invented on this Earth,
> Its animated marvel makes you duck
> For all your worth

And so on, through the crowded, rocking night, the songs soon giving way to dancing in the limited space on the limestone floor. Old-fashioned waltzes, seven-step polkas, schottisches, and the Four-Handed Reel, our boots clumping on the stones as we twirl and spin and clap hands. How lucky we are to be so far from towns! This must be one of the last villages in Dorset where the old dances are danced naturally, without any help from urban country-lovers who can only succeed in making our dances precious and setting the ploughmen against them.

And the year died towards Christmas, through muck-spreading and ploughing and sowing of the winter corn, and the ghostly lights of milkers' bicycles coming down the hill to the dairy before break of day, their tyres crackling on the thin ice of puddles in the road. One night, as I sit by the fire in my ancient house marooned in the fields, I hear from the dark night a first faint preliminary wheeze, a few quavering notes growing to full volume of treble and cracking alto voices of the carol-singers: 'While shepherd watched their flocks by night'.

And I fling open the door, and distribute my loose change to the waits standing there, with the publican's daughter carrying a lantern; and they sing 'God rest ye merry gentlemen' and go on to the next farm. And later, I wander up to the dairy, where the cows are breathing sweet and heavy in their straw, and occasionally a chain clanks in the warm darkness, and I wonder if any of them are on their knees, as in the legend, remembering the words of our gentle poet of these fields, Tom Hardy:

If someone said on Christmas Eve,
'Come; see the oxen kneel
In the lonely barton by yonder coomb
Our childhood used to know,'
I would go with him in the gloom,
Hoping it might be so.

A Victorian Christmas card.

Burning the Holly
By Thomas Hardy

✳

Twelfth Night ends the Christmas celebration, when the greenery is burnt or thrown away. Traditionally it is a time of parting and pairing up and the earliest of the Twelfth Nights mentioned in the poem does give fruition to a relationship; but the lady returns two years later on Twelfth Night with a child and without her lover.

John Udal says that Twelfth Night is 'the last day upon which it is lawful to eat mince pies, which are essentially a Christmas dish. To eat one on each of the twelve days of Christmas is said to ensure for the eater entire happiness for the ensuing year, or, failing that, one happy month for each mince-pie so eaten. In some parts of Dorsetshire, however, it is said that to procure the desired result each mince-pie must be of a different person's 'make', or must be eaten at a different house.

The poem is from Thomas Hardy's Winter Words *collection (published posthumously in 1928).*

> O you are sad on Twelfth Night,
> I notice: sad on Twelfth Night;
> You are as sad on Twelfth Night
> As any that I know.
>
> 'Yes: I am sad on that night,
> Doubtless I'm sad on that night:
> Yes; I am sad on that night,
> For we all loved her so!'

'Burning the Greens' from *Harper's Weekly*, 1876.

Why are you sad on Twelfth Night,
Especially on Twelfth Night?
Why are you sad on Twelfth Night
When wit and laughter flow?

– 'She'd been a famous dancer,
Much lured of men; a dancer.
She'd been a famous dancer,
Facile in heel and toe.

'And we were burning the holly
On Twelfth Night; the holly,
As people do: the holly,
Ivy, and mistletoe.

'And while it popped and crackled,
(She being our lodger), crackled;
And while it popped and crackled,
Her face caught by the glow,

'In he walked and said to her,
In a slow voice he said to her;
Yes, walking in he said to her,
'We sail before cock-crow.'

'Why did you not come on to me,
As promised? Yes, come on to me?
Why did you not come on to me,
Since you had sworn to go?

'His eyes were deep and flashing,
As flashed the holm-flames: flashing;
His eyes were deep, and flashing
In their quick, keen upthrow.

'As if she had been ready,
Had furtively been ready;
As if she had been ready
For his insistence – lo! –

'She clasped his arm and went with him
As his entirely: went with him.
She clasped his arm and went with him
Into the sprinkling snow.

'We saw the prickly leaves waste
To ashes: saw the leaves waste;
The burnt-up prickly leaves waste
The pair had gone also.

– 'On Twelfth Night, two years after –
Yes, Twelfth Night, two years after;
On Twelfth Night, two years after,
We sat – our spirits low –

'Musing, when back the door swung
Without a knock. The door swung;
Thought flew to her. The door swung,
And in she came, pale, slow;

'Against her breast a child clasped;
Close to her breast a child clasped;
She stood there with the clasped,
Swaying it to and fro.

'Her look alone the tale told;
Quite wordless was the tale told;
Her careworn eyes the tale told
As larger they seemed to grow.

'One day next spring she disappeared,
The second time she disappeared.
And that time, when she'd disappeared
Came back no more. Ah, no!

'But we still burn the holly
On Twelfth Night; burn the holly
As people do: the holly,
Ivy, and mistletoe.'